Was on my heart to bless you with this devotional.

Pray you are greatly be encouraged!

PRAYER MATTERS

The Transforming Power of Persevering and Believing Prayer

Love & Prayers

Shannon Bryant

Shannon Bryant

Copyright © 2016 Shannon Bryant
All rights reserved.
Contact author on Facebook or email: Shannon.bryant1@aol.com
ISBN: 1533133735
ISBN 13: 9781533133731

Marshall, I thank you for believing in me. You are a man of great, unwavering faith, and I'm blessed to have spent over half my life with you in marriage. Your prayers, love, and support have always been consistent and unchanging. Without your cheering me on every step of the way, my dream of writing Prayer Matters *would've remained a seed unplanted, and for that I am forever grateful.*

Unless otherwise noted, all scripture quotations are taken from the New King James Version of the Bible.

Cover design by Shanise Bryant

CONTENTS

Introduction	ix
Taste and See That the Lord Is Good!	1
Jesus Left Us Peace	8
Filled with Joy	18
Firm Faith	27
Divine Guidance	38
Hope in God	45
Prayer Life	53
Pathway to Freedom	63
God Will Supply	72
Godly Wisdom	80
Moving Forward	88
God's Call	97
Self-Control	105
God's Unfailing Love	118
Strength in Difficult Times	126
Altogether Beautiful	138
Running on Empty	149
Don't Be Afraid	159
Right Relationships	168
A Life Hidden with Christ	184

INTRODUCTION

The righteous cry out, and the Lord hears them, He delivers them from all their troubles.

—Psalms 34:17

Trusting God in the difficult times can be quite challenging. In this world of uncertainty, violence, marital problems, problems with children, financial problems, sickness, depression, disappointments—the list can go on and on—life can get downright overbearing and overwhelming, to say the least. Sometimes the burdens seem too heavy to bear. Sometimes you feel like your heart aches and you can't find peace or comfort. Even at times when you don't have the words, when it's just a moan, groan, or a sigh, you cry out to God. Your heart's cry is, "Lord, I need Your embrace, right at this moment. Let me know that everything is going to be OK. Lord, I can't make it without you. I need Your strength to make it through. Lord, I don't even know what to do or which way to go. Lord, when will my healing come? I've been sick for so long."

Shannon Bryant

When you cry out to Him and He seems silent, do you have the assurance in your hearts that He hears you? In those dreadful times when you feel alone and that no one cares or even understands, do you stand on His promise that He will never leave you nor forsake you? Whatever the circumstance, in these critical days of unrest and uncertainty our faith must be uplifted and unwavering—trusting Him to do all and to be all, in and through us. You must have the confidence in knowing that though at times you may be crushed in spirit, He hears you, and He will bring you out. He loves you; He cares for you; He is listening; He is faithful! The true and living God is willing and eager to answer your heart's cry. Trust Him more fully in this very moment. Believe God will do just what He says. He will give you peace, comfort, direction, and healing. He will supply your every need His way, according to His will, by His timing, and for His glory. May you persevere in prayer and wait patiently on the Lord for your prayers to be manifested. Inviting God into your situation through persevering and believing prayer will not only transform you, but it will transform your life and others' lives that your life touches. Prayer matters.

Trust in Him at all times, you people; Pour out your heart before Him; God is a refuge for us.

—Psalms 62:8

TASTE AND SEE THAT THE LORD IS GOOD!

Taste and see that the Lord is good; blessed is the one who takes refuge in Him.

—Psalms 34:80

Taste and see! In the natural realm I often taste and see—food, that is. To be honest, I taste *too* often at times. I'm still a work in progress. But I do enjoy a delicious, well-prepared meal that makes my taste buds dance.

Once I was invited over to a good friend of mine's house for dinner. I looked at the dinner table, which featured a large spread of very appetizing cuisine. It looked like it was going to send my taste buds into the "running man" dance. The food was perfectly plated, tempting, and very pretty—almost too pretty to eat. My mouth started to water as I anticipated how good this food was going to taste. In my mind I thought, "I hope it tastes as good as it looks." My hopes were high as I finally tasted the meal.

To my surprise, it was horrible! I looked around to see if anyone saw my face as I tried to hide my distaste. I'm so transparent that I'm sure my facial expression showed my displeasure at the food. I've always worn my feelings on my face, and I couldn't hide my feelings if I tried. I would never want to offend anyone, especially after they put all that hard work into preparing a meal. My mind started to reflect on when I was a little girl and hadn't finished all of the food that was on my plate. My dad would always say, "You better eat all of that food. There are children starving in Africa who would love to have that food!" So I did nibble around the plate a bit before carefully and conspicuously covering the plate with a napkin. But I did ask myself, "How could something look so good yet taste so bad?" My eyes had deceived me.

Now I invite you to join me in a supernatural tasting, a spiritual feast! God has prepared a table before us. And guess what? Our enemies will even be there (Ps. 23:5). God will anoint our heads with oil and our cups will run over. God is the Host, and we can have our fill of everything on the table. Because God is the Host, we know for sure that everything on His table is good. On His table there is no unsavory food; it looks good, tastes good, and is good for us, for God is good! His spiritual food is favorable and superb: "How sweet are Your Words to my taste, sweeter than honey to my mouth" (Ps. 119:103). He is our Shepherd, and we shall not want. In His presence is the fullness of joy to receive as our hearts desire. How great it is to dine with our Heavenly Father!

I have not always eaten at the Lord's table. Although there has always been an open invitation to dine with the Lord, I declined His offer for a long time. In the past I thought I had surrendered all to God, but there were areas of my life that I needed to let go of but I just wasn't ready. See, I wasn't attracted to the Lord's table because the table didn't fit my taste at the time. I still had a taste for the world and fleshly desires. I had no problem being holy Monday through Thursday. When I would get off of work Fridays, the party would begin and usually ended late Saturday night. Oh, but I did manage to get up, fix breakfast, get the kids together, get myself together, and go to church on Sundays. Just sitting there in the pew, empty, hungover, and convicted. I desperately needed to exchange my desires for God's desires. I needed to clean off my plate and load up on what God had to offer me. I was getting tired of disappointing God and myself. My taste needed to change as soon as possible, but it would still be a while before any real change took place in my life.

I started drinking at the age of fourteen. It started with an innocent little taste of wine. The wine was so sweet and fragrant, and it went down so smooth. So delicious, no harm in it, besides it tasted like juice. Little did I know that this would be the beginning of a battle that I struggled to win for a long time. Wine and strong drink became my pleasure and my crutch. I loved the taste and I loved the feeling that it gave me. It numbed my pain and to be honest, it just made me feel good. For years I sought after that good feeling. That false sense of happiness, comfort, peace, and "liquid confidence".

The bible warns in Proverbs 23:30-32, "Those who linger long at the wine, those who go in search of mixed wine. Do not look on the wine when it is red, when it sparkles in the cup, when it swirls around smoothly; at the last it bites like a serpent and stings like a viper." This scripture is not talking about people who can have a glass of wine or two then stop. This scripture is talking about me and people like me who can't stop at just one or two. People who linger long at wine or other alcohol and go in search of it. People who feel they have to have it to cope with life. We are not to even look at it. Although it sparkles, it may taste good, and makes us feel good for a moment, it is a mocker. (Proverbs 20:1) Alcohol definitely made a fool of me until I got fed up with misery.

I began to seek the Lord and attempt to clean up my life. You know like when you were a kid and you'd have to go wash up before you could come to the table and eat. That's what I thought I had to do before going to the table that God had prepared. I thought I had to get myself together, clean my life up, and I would be most presentable to dine with the Lord. After years of trying and failing in my own strength, I yielded to God and asked for His help. God began to change my life, not instantly it was a process of depending on Him to do what I couldn't do on my own. I found out that I couldn't clean myself up, and that it was never a requirement from God for me to do so. God loved me just the way I was but He didn't want me to stay that way, and He was going to help me. When I had a true revelation of God's love for me, my life began to transform. My taste began to change.

I began to crave the Word of God. God would speak to me through reading the bible and the scriptures were alive, and active. It was if God was speaking directly to my heart. All the places that were broken He began to mend so perfectly and completely. God replaced hurt, feelings of rejection from my past, guilt and shame, with a huge heaping helping of His grace and goodness at His table. Rather than being filled with worry, and anxiety God gave me extra helpings of peace and comfort. Instead of craving alcohol, I began to thirst for His Living Water that quenched and saturated my innermost being. Nothing else would satisfy. See, God knew what I needed. He knows what we have need of before we ask Him. (Matthew 6:8) He just wants us to accept His invitation. To spend time with Him, get to know Him and receive all the essential spiritual food we need to be healed and made whole in Him. Everything we need is already pre-prepared at His glorious table.

At this magnificent table is all that we will ever need and long for. We can taste of His love, grace, goodness, mercy, and kindness. All the nourishment that we need is set out before us in plenty. If you are deficient in peace, it's at the table, so take a double portion if you need it. If you are lacking hope, partake of it. If you need comfort, He has the ultimate comfort food: spiritual food. The Holy Spirit, the Comforter, will fill you up to overflow. At this buffet that the Lord has prepared is all the nourishment you need to make you spiritually strong and healthy. As you begin to taste of this divine feast, you desire more and more, and the more you eat of it, the stronger you get.

There is great abundance at this holy feast. You never have to be concerned about running out; it's from everlasting to everlasting. There is always more than enough. The more we taste of His goodness, the more we want of Him. Our desires will be to spend more time with Him and abide in Him. Communion with our Heavenly Father is a marvelous fellowship, as He is the Vine and we are the branches. The Vine nourishes the branches, holds the branches up, supports them, and makes the branches strong. As we rest in Him, He gives us all we need to grow, be healthy, and bear more fruit (John 15:5).

As we abide in Him, our tastes begin to change. The things that used to taste good don't taste good anymore. Bitterness, resentment, anger, and sin no longer suit our taste buds anymore, and we want to spit them out. They contaminate our lives and are poison to our souls. Instead, we start to crave more of the Living God. As we delight ourselves in Him, He gives us His desires: "Delight yourself also in the Lord, and He will give you the desires of your heart" (Ps. 37:4). When the desires of our hearts come from the Lord, He will give them to us. Taste and see the goodness of the Lord! His spiritual food will heal, refresh, revive, restore, and give you the endurance and perseverance you need to live a victorious life. Taste and see His goodness. It's critical to partake

5

of all that the Lord offers us. It promotes good spiritual health and prevents spiritual sickness. Partake from His goodness daily; it's essential. There is more than enough. You can't take too much of God's spiritual food. We are to be full of His Spirit, filled with His full glory (Acts 13:52). Get your fill of all that the Lord has for you. Continually taste and see the goodness of the Lord. Go back over and over to get your fill. It's to your benefit to be spiritually obese. The more you partake, the more joy and peace you will have. You will be wiser and stronger, and God's power will give you the endurance and perseverance to run the race that God has set before you. It's an all-you-can-eat buffet of His gloriousness! Always give compliments, thanks, glory, and praise to the One who prepared it for the nourishment of our spirit.

Prayer Matter

Father, in the name of Jesus, I thank You that You have prepared a table before me. May I respond with a greater Yes to Your invitation to partake of Your goodness. I thank You that as I partake I will get stronger and have more endurance and perseverance to run the race You have set before me. Grow me, Lord, into a yielding, pure vessel to be used for Your glory.

Everlasting Father, may my desires be in alignment with Yours. Lord, sometimes I want what is not good for me; please take those desires away. I pray my palate will begin to change. It is my heart's desire to crave righteousness, more of You, more of Your Holy Spirit. May I feed on Your every word. Awaken my spiritual taste buds to only things that will nourish, replenish, and strengthen my inner man. May I have an overflow of Your peace, joy, love, and goodness.

Forgive me, Lord, when I get discouraged and want to give up or turn back to old habits. Forgive me, Lord, when I want to wallow in self-pity or succumb to the turmoil of guilt and condemnation. I know all these things are from the enemy of my soul and are a sign that I need to spend more time with You. May I hunger and thirst for holiness, knowing I will never be satisfied until I've had my fill of You. Lord, as I come to partake

Prayer Matters

of Your spiritual feast, may I always be mindful not to just think of myself. It is required of me to invite others to partake of Your saving grace. There is always more than enough and it's free. Jesus paid it all. In Jesus's name I pray, amen.

JESUS LEFT US PEACE

Peace I leave with you; my peace I give to you; I do not give as the world gives. Do not let your hearts be troubled and do not be afraid.

—John 14:27

Peace is a rich, spiritual gift that was left here for us by our Lord and Savior Jesus Christ. This spiritual fruit was left here for us by Jesus because He knew that we would have a dire need for it. The world around us in in total chaos. What was once wrong is right, and what was once right is wrong. The pressures and stresses we have today have us longing for the peace of God. If peace was given to us, then why are so many people suffering from depression, anxiety, panic attacks, despair, hopelessness, insomnia, and suicidal thoughts? We have an enemy who is determined to steal, kill and destroy us (John 10:10). I am thankful to God that we are not left to ourselves. God has given us everything we need to live a victorious life through Him.

Prayer Matters

In military combat, the enemy tends to strike at the most important points. So too does the enemy of our souls. A major point of entry for Satan to attack is our minds. He will use blockades; he wants you to cut off communication to God and others, which in turn leads to isolation. He will come at you head-on, or he may have an indirect attack through others. If he can't get to you, he'll use your spouse, children, job, etc. Deception is on one of his main weapons. This strategy seeks to trick and give false perceptions. The enemy attacks our minds with negative thoughts contrary to the Word of God. If the enemy can attack our thought lives, spiritual strongholds will develop within us. Whatever it may be will have such a "strong hold" on you and you will have no control over it. Only by the power of God can you have victory in that area. I have personally been attacked in my mind with fear, depression, anxiety, insecurities, and deception. Addiction had a strong hold on me. These were all weapons that the enemy used to discourage me, exhaust me, and cause me to have feelings of giving up. I thought, "Why keep trying if I keep messing up, doing the same things, making the wrong choices? God is not pleased with me. I'm never going to get it right." Yes, condemnation oppressed me for a long time. To say I beat myself up is an understatement. I allowed the enemy to get in my head and in my feelings. He was lying to me and I believed him. These lies from Satan kept me right where he wanted me to be: in bondage and not in the will of God for my life.

The world offers peace and comfort in the form of bad relationships, drugs, alcohol, worldly music, shopping, overeating, hoarding, social media, and the list goes on. There are all kinds of substitutes for what we really need, and that is a true relationship with Jesus Christ. My substitute for peace for a long time was found in a bottle: alcohol. As I mentioned earlier the alcohol numbed my past and the hurt I was feeling at the time, and it seemed to calm my anxieties. The alcohol also gave me a false sense of happiness. But when I sobered up, the emotional pain and anxiety I felt

9

came back and came back even worse, accompanied by hangovers. The temporary false sense of happiness was replaced with more depression and torment in my mind because now I had to deal with shame before God. Condemnation would soon set in. Then I would have to pray the same prayer that I'd prayed, which seemed like a million times. "Lord, forgive me, deliver me, and set me free." Yes, and the most used one, I'm ashamed to say, was "I'll never get drunk again." In my heart, I wanted to please Him and walk in obedience. My spirit was willing, but my flesh was weak. In my heart, I loved the Lord and wanted to please Him. Condemnation, guilt, and shame began to take a hold of me, and this started a downward spiral in my life that went on for years. All my years of me "disappointing" God led me to believe that He didn't love me. I thought that I had to earn God's love. I thought that if I was living right, He'd love me, and that if I messed up, He'd stop loving me. I now recognize that was a lie from the enemy.

I'm so thankful that I now know that while God was not pleased with my sin, He still loved me. When I got that revelation of God's love for me, my journey to freedom began. I didn't have to work to be right with God because I was already right with God. The Bible tells us in Isaiah 64:6, "But we are all like an unclean thing. And all our righteousness are like filthy rags." On our own we have no righteousness, and only through placing our faith in Jesus have we been made right with God (Rom. 3:22–26). Do I fall short? Yes, but I don't keep count anymore. God doesn't, so why should I (Heb. 8:12)? If I confess my sins to Him, He is just and faithful to forgive me, and the bonus is that He cleanses me from all unrighteousness (1 John 1:9). I never had a real understanding of God's grace. I never have to work for grace—it's free. I don't have to make myself loved by God; I am loved by God, and that's it. Jesus paid for my sins, and I am redeemed.

I remember one morning, after a weekend of heavy drinking, I cried out to God. I mean sobbing, snot everywhere, an emotional wreck, full of shame. After a weekend binge, I would feel so guilty and ashamed, I couldn't stand myself. So after I finally built up enough courage to go to God, I cried out with a heavy heart, "Lord, forgive me. I need Your help. I can't do this alone. Please forgive me. I'm so ashamed." "Lord forgive me, and help me to forgive myself." God spoke to me so clearly, not audibly, but in my spirit. He said, "Who do you think you are that you can't forgive yourself? I am the God of all mankind and if I can forgive you, who do you think you are? Do you think you are more than God Almighty? If I can forgive you, you can certainly forgive yourself." I was immediately humbled. I believe God was telling me in so many words that not forgiving myself is a form of pride, wallowing in self-pity and guilt for a self-inflicted wound that I had made. Alcohol had me bound and I needed to be let loose. It took making a decision, not an emotional experience. I've had so many emotional experiences at the altar, thinking I was really giving it over to God. Only in a matter of weeks I'd pick it back up again. I had to make a decision to not drink and ask God to help. I had to come to the point that I'm not playing with God anymore. Furthermore, He is not playing with me. Time is winding up; my life is at stake, and the lives of others I am to affect for Him are at stake. It's not just an emotional experience—it's a decision to give it to God, and not to take it back, and when you feel like you are tempted, praying, reading the Bible, and having someone you trust hold you accountable is great. God loves us so much that He always provides a way of escape for us (1 Cor. 10:13). I thank God for the way and for giving me the strength to take it. We can have peace in knowing that in place of what we deserve, He blesses us and gives us love, grace, and mercy.

God led me to a scripture one morning and it spoke to me, like it was from God's heart to mine. The scripture was from Psalm 51:6, it says, "Behold You desire truth in the inward parts, and in the hidden part You will make me to know wisdom." I knew that

God needed for me to be honest with myself and more importantly I needed to be honest with Him. See, on the outside I was functional, happy marriage, for the most part well -mannered children, and a nice home. I laugh now but I remember some people would call us the "Huxtables". On the outside looking in everything seemed fine, but on the inside I was struggling with depression, anxiety attacks and alcohol abuse. I could hide these things well from people, but I couldn't hide from God. He sees all even into the innermost parts of our minds and hearts. God required for me to be honest with Him and myself and only then would He make me to know wisdom. I was coming out of darkness into the light and God had my hand. He was leading me and helping me every step of the way. Only when I took off the mask and sincerely opened my heart up to God did true healing, peace and deliverance come into my life.

"The thief does not come except to steal, kill, and destroy. I have come that they may have life, and that they may have it more abundantly" (John 10:10). Satan tries to steal everything the Lord gave to you. If you let the thief in, he'll steal your peace, joy, and hope. Romans 12:2 reads, "And do not be conformed to this world, but be transformed by the renewing of your mind, that you may prove what is that good and acceptable and perfect will of God." The enemy counterattacks by planting beliefs and ideas in your mind contrary to the Word of God. The enemy is a liar and a deceiver. That is why it is so important to read, know, understand, and meditate on the Word of God.

God has the ammunition and has provided us with weapons of warfare to win!

For though we walk in the flesh, we do not war according to the flesh. For the weapons of warfare are not carnal, but mighty in God for pulling down strongholds, casting down

Prayer Matters

arguments and every high thing that exalts itself against the knowledge of God, bringing every thought into captivity to the obedience of Christ. (2 Cor. 10:3–5)

A most powerful weapon is the Sword of the Spirit, the Word of God. It's sharper than any two-edged sword (Heb. 4:12). Think about sharper than any two-edged sword. Two-edges makes the sword easier to permeate. The Word of God is sharp which makes it easier to touch the heart of those who read and receive it. Study and meditate on the Word of God. By meditating on the scriptures, you are renewing your mind. God's thoughts become your thoughts. Meditate on them day and night. This uplifts your faith. A scripture that helped me tremendously was Philippians 4:8 ("Finally, brethren, whatever things are true, whatever things are noble, whatever things are just, whatever things are pure, whatever things are lovely, whatever things are of good report, if there is anything praiseworthy—meditate on these things"). If what you are thinking about does not involve any of the things mentioned in this verse, try your best by the power of the Holy Spirit to throw it out of your mind. The enemy has to be stopped at the door! That means that as soon as a thought that is contrary to the Word of God comes into your mind, throw it out! Don't give the enemy an entryway into your mind. If he finds a crack in the door, he'll eventually come all the way in. Don't allow him to do that. When bad thoughts come into your mind, replace them with the Word of God. When you're afraid and fear begins to overtake you, say, "God has not given me a spirit of fear, but of power and love and of a sound mind" (2 Tim. 1:7). When you feel like giving up and you're losing hope, say, "I can do all things through Christ who strengthens me" (Phil. 4:13). Find a scripture that fits your current situation, read it, pray it, and believe it.

When our minds are not protected by the Word of God, we have weak entry points, where Satan will enter in. When we are weak, he will sneak. When you are going through a trial, this is the time go deeper in scripture and prayer. I know sometimes it can be hard, but keep pressing, for your victory is sure. May your mind be so filled with the Word of God that there won't be any room for the enemy to enter in. The Word of God is a "deadbolt lock" on the door of your mind so the enemy cannot gain access.

Let the Word of God be saturated in your mouth, mind, and heart. Jesus combated the enemy with the Word of God when He was tempted in the wilderness. Jesus had just fasted for forty days and forty nights, and He was hungry.

The enemy tempts Him by saying, "If You are the Son of God, command that these stones become bread" (Matt. 4:3). In verse 4, Jesus answers, "It is written, Man shall not live by bread alone, but by every word that proceeds out of the mouth of God." Jesus is tempted three times in the wilderness. The first point I notice here is that Satan uses a time that he thought Jesus would be weak. Jesus had been fasting for forty days and forty nights, and the enemy picks this time to tempt Jesus with food because Jesus is hungry (Matt. 4:2). He uses the same tactic with us—to get us when we are weak or maybe when we are going through a tough time. This is often when the enemy will try to bombard your mind with lies, negative thoughts, and emotions. When you are weak, he will sneak and tempt you with things and in areas that he knows in the past you have struggled with. But Jesus gives us a perfect example to follow. Three times Jesus is tempted in the wilderness. Each time His response is to quote the Word of God. There is so much power in the Word of God! The Word of God is the ammunition, "the nuclear bomb," to destroy the works of the enemy.

Pray without ceasing! "Be anxious for nothing, but in everything by prayer and supplications, with thanksgiving, let your requests be made known to God; and the peace of God will guard your hearts and minds through Christ Jesus" (Phil. 4:8). God gives us everything we need to get where He wants us to be. Anxiety is

Prayer Matters

so prevalent in today's society. Paul exhorts here to be anxious for nothing! Pray, commit your problems to the Lord, and trust Him for deliverance. Be thankful in your prayers as you tell God about all that you need and then the peace of God will guard your heart and your mind. To guard our minds means to protect them. And how do you protect your mind? Read the Bible, renew your mind, and put on the helmet of salvation. The helmet of salvation must be put on to protect our minds and to help us to discern the truth from the lies and deception of the enemy (Eph. 6:17). This head-gear is mandatory to guard our minds and thoughts through God's saving grace. If you are in Christ, your salvation is sure. Satan will try to bombard your mind with discouragement and doubt, but when you have that helmet on, you are protected from the lies, and you can have assurance and hope that all things will work together for your good (Rom. 8:28). Then we will be able to bring every thought into captivity to the obedience of Christ (2 Cor. 11:5b).

Finally, praise God for the victory! Praise God even when you are in difficult circumstances. This requires a sacrifice sometimes. Because when you are going through the hard times, you don't "feel" like praising Him. Oh, but there is no better place to praise than when you are in a hard place. Even if you don't feel like it, push yourself to praise. This won't make any sense to the enemy, and in fact it will baffle him (2 Chron. 20:21–22). Praise gets our minds off of our problems and our focus on God and His sovereignty, knowing that He is in control and the battle is won already. He will put a Word in your heart and give you the assurance that He is with you! Praise Him like you have already come out of the situation! Your victory is sure, but that does not mean that you don't have to fight.

In a boxing match, one boxer may be favored to win. People may say that one fighter is a sure win over the other: "The fight is already won! It's going to be a knockout." Although one boxer is sure to win, they both still have to fight the fight. Only one will come out victorious, receive the championship belt, and be labeled the "champ." With God, the fight is fixed. That does not mean that we don't fight. God will do His part, but we have to do our part also by listening to His word, praying, praising, worshipping, and being obedient. With God on our side, God in us, God with us, and God for us, we can be sure we will come out winners! We don't get a championship belt for a spiritual fight; we get the garment of praise for our spirit of heaviness, the oil of joy for mourning, and beauty for ashes (Isa. 61:3)! We can live victorious lives now, and have lives of peace. The same mind that is in Christ Jesus will be in us (Phil. 2:5). Even more, in glory we will receive our crowns of life in heaven that the Lord has promised to those who love Him (James 1:12).

Prayer Matter

Father, I thank You for leaving Your precious gift of peace for me to receive. Lord, You are my Peace. You said in Your Word that I don't have to be troubled or afraid. Lord, I thank You that You are always with me (John 14:27). I pray that You will put a hedge of protection around my mind so that the enemy cannot enter in, so I won't be deceived in any area, especially in my thought process.

May I meditate on Your Word, pray Your Word, say Your Word, and be a doer of Your Word. May Your Word strengthen and discipline me for the fight. I know the fight is surely won because You are fighting for me and with me.

Help me to always be mindful of what I allow in my mind through television, books, Internet, and words of others. If these things are not edifying, then give me wisdom, revelation, and strength let go of anything that is not pleasing in Your sight. Reveal to me areas where I have allowed negative mind-sets, ideas, and concepts to creep in my mind. Turn away my eyes from looking at worthless things, and revive me in Your way (Ps. 119:37).

Father, free me from worry, anxiety, depression, fear, condemnation, and torment. Instead, I ask for an outpouring of Your Holy Spirit upon me

Prayer Matters

to help, comfort, and strengthen me. Enable me to take every thought captive to the obedience of Jesus Christ (1 Cor. 10:5). I pray that the same mind that is in Christ Jesus be in me (Phil. 2:5). Help me to always cast my care upon You. When the cares of this world start to overwhelm me, help me not to be consumed. I put my trust in You.

I put on the helmet of salvation to protect my mind from deception and the lies of the enemy. Your saving grace is the blockade to destroy and annihilate his plan to capture my mind. Lord, I pray that my mind be so occupied by You that the enemy has no room to come in and torture it. I know it is your will that I know and experience the fullness of Your perfect peace that surpasses all understanding. I know that if I keep my mind fixed on You, You will keep me in perfect peace (Isa. 26:3). Father, release into me a spring of Your overflowing, never-ending, perfect peace. I look away from the circumstance and I look to You, Lord. Thank You for Your precious gift of peace. I receive it. Nothing is missing, and nothing is broken. In Jesus's name I pray, amen.

FILLED WITH JOY

Now may the God of hope fill you with all joy and peace in believing, that you may abound in hope by the power of the Holy Spirit.

—Romans 15:13

We've all heard the saying that happiness is based on our circumstances, but joy is from the Lord. This is a true and proven statement. But how do we maintain our joy in the midst of what I like to call "AT&T" (adversities, trials, and tribulations)? Oh, it's easy to say we have the joy of the Lord when everything is fine, but what about when we are going through the hard times? When things seem to be happening consecutively, one situation after another? When your teenager is rebelling and going against everything you have taught him? Bills are long and money is short. When you are caregiving for your parent

Prayer Matters

or a loved, grieving, going through a bitter divorce, how do you maintain and keep your joy? As difficult as it may seem to be, it is possible. Although in our flesh we may hurt, I call these "flesh wounds." Our inner man will still have a peace and joy, knowing that God is going to work everything out for our good. We can have the assurance that weeping may endure for a night, but joy will come in the morning (Ps. 30:5) and that though in times we may sow in tears, we shall reap with joy (Ps. 126:5). Difficult circumstances can rob us of our joy, but by the power of God through faith, we can maintain joy-filled lives.

Getting into the presence of God is very important in order to have the fullness of joy (Ps. 16:11). There lies in His presence an unspeakable, unexplainable joy. Praying, worshipping, and crying out to God from the depths of your heart releases the joy of the Lord. This gladness given by God is found when you spend time with Him. He lets you know that you have the choice and privilege of casting your cares on Him. And once you cast them on Him, don't take them back. Worrying implies that you think that you still have control over the matter. He is in control; trust Him to work it out all out for your good. Prayer moves God's hand, and it's best if we don't move until we have direction from God. We have hope knowing that He is intervening on our behalf, and His hope does not disappoint. While you are at rest in your spirit knowing that He's working it out, the joy of the Lord will be your strength and your confidence will be in Him, not in you trying to make moves without the prompting of the Holy Spirit. When God works out that situation, what a joy you will have.

If we have no joy, we have no strength: "The joy of the Lord is your strength" (Neh. 8:10b). When we are in Him, God places this joy in our heart. I mean, this joy is special, and you can only get it from God. You can't find it anywhere else. You can't find it in the world, money, houses, careers, or substances. Joy of the Lord is not found in external things. External things are temporary and for a moment; joy is eternal and inside of our hearts. He can touch a heart like no other. He will give you gladness where sadness used to reside, and all you have to do is invite Him into your heart and into your situation and then receive joy by faith (Ps. 4:7).

There are some things that will block the flow of joy in your life. Not living according to His ways will interrupt the joy flow. Deliberately practicing sin stops the blessing of joy from your life. I know this from my own experience. At times in my life when I had not been living according to the Word of God, "doing my own thing," I was miserable. I thought I was having fun at the time, but afterward I was downright pathetic and depressed. I thank God that He never let me be comfortable in sin. I was never content, and my flesh was weak. I had these standards set for myself and when I missed the mark, I would withdraw and allow guilt and condemnation to depress me. I had no joy, and my spiritual growth was halted. I felt like every time I messed up, I had to start all over, like going back to the starting line in a race. I knew God loved me, but as I got to know Him more, I knew He expected more from me, and when I didn't do what I knew what was right in God's eyes, I was not happy and felt like a failure. Yes, the Holy Spirit would convict me, but I lived in condemnation. I thought I had to make myself right, while not knowing that God had already made me right with Him.

My cycle of condemnation, guilt, shame, depression, and discouragement originated from me being involved in a doctrine driven by "works," fear, and control. I thought my salvation was based on my capabilities to live righteously and not break the rules. This misplaced confidence in myself and my abilities would lead me and keep me in a constant state of defeat. I was always struggling to live a perfect life while always missing the mark.

Growing up and even well into adulthood, I lived in a continual state of fear. I was fearful of the world ending and me being destroyed, of my family lives being lost who were not in the same denomination, and of not being accepted by my family who were. I also had an unhealthy fear of God: fear of not being able to live up to all the rules and conditions. If I didn't live up to what God expected of me, He would be angry and not be pleased with me, and I would be punished. I didn't know God as a loving and merciful God. My perception of God was off, mainly because I didn't have a personal relationship with Him and because of what I was taught in relation to God. I was so sin conscious. If I lived right, I felt love and accepted by God and others. If I messed up, I felt rejected by God and others. I believe that the rejection I felt and cutting off communication was a form of control so that I could get back in line with what was being taught. So in order to be accepted, loved, and not be destroyed, I worked hard to live a godly life—only to fail. I would aim high and miss the mark sometimes. When I did miss the mark—because that is what imperfect people do sometimes—I would get depressed and frustrated. I was so consumed with guilt and condemnation all the time because I couldn't live up to what was expected of me. This kept me in a state of hopelessness. The only way I felt accepted and loved by God and by people in the religion was if I was doing the "works" that I was taught. See, I was working to gain love, acceptance, and salvation, mostly out of fear and rejection. I didn't know that I didn't have to work for these things; these things had already been freely given to me by God, and all I had to do was receive them. It doesn't make sense to work for a free gift, just accept it and say, "Thank You Lord!"

Only when I started reading and studying the Bible for myself did God start to open my spiritual eyes to His truths in the Word. The words in the Bible started to come alive and God was speaking to my heart personally. God began to open my eyes and give me understanding. The bible says that the Holy Spirit will guide you into all truth. (John 16:13) I asked the Holy Spirit to give me a greater understanding of the word of God. Through prayer, studying the Bible, and being taught sound doctrine, I found out that Jesus is the Way, the Truth, and the Life. Jesus was not downplayed anymore. He is the Savior, Redeemer, and every tongue shall confess that He is Lord (Phil. 2:11)! No one comes to the Father except through Him (John 14:6). We will stand before the judgment seat of Christ (Rom. 14:10b). I learned that Jesus died for my sins and I have been redeemed from the curse of the law by Jesus" (Gal. 3:13). The scripture says in 2 Corinthians 3:5–6, "Not that we are sufficient of ourselves to think of anything as being from ourselves, but our sufficiency is from God, who also made us sufficient as ministers of the new covenant, not of the letter but of the Spirit; for the letter kills, but the Spirit gives life." The letter kills because nobody can live up to it. The law brings attention to sin and death. Jesus came so that we may have life and have it more abundantly, and that includes salvation (John 10:10). We are saved by grace through faith (Eph. 2:8), a free gift given by God. This undeserving gift of the power of the Holy Spirit touches our hearts, giving us life and transforming us for His glory. The Holy Spirit enlightened my eyes so I could understand, and He freed me from such an enormous boulder of burden. I was no longer weighed down, and I responded to Jesus's call, "Come to Me, all you who labor and are heavy laden, and I will give you rest. For My yoke is easy and my burden is light" (Matt. 11:28, 30). You see, I wasn't meant to carry the burden; Jesus had already carried it for me when He gave His life for me (Rom. 4:25). In Christ I am free, for there is no condemnation to those who are in Christ Jesus (Rom. 8:1a).

In my continued studying of the Bible I began to study the life of Jesus. Jesus is our example so of course in order to be a close follower of Him, we have to know Him and know about how He lived His life, especially in relation to servanthood. I loved the fact that the religion stressed evangelism, which is what we all are commanded to do. To go out and proclaim the good news of the gospel of Jesus Christ.

Prayer Matters

Although evangelism was their main focus, I began to take notice of their servanthood to people outside of their religion. I never saw community outreaches to help others in need. For example: most churches have outreaches. These outreaches and ministries are used to feed the hungry, clothe the poor, visit the hospitals and pray for the sick, visit prisons and more. Though the goal here is to meet a need, the primary and most important goal is to share the good news of the gospel, bring people to Christ, and give people hope. Yes, we are to take care of the household of God but we should also show compassion and meet the needs of the poor and less fortunate. (Gal. 6:10) It's in the giving of ourselves that we have the opportunity to give others hope. Hope to not just some people but all who will have an ear to hear and a heart to receive. The Bible says in Matthew 5:16, "Let your light so shine before men, that they may see your good works and glorify your Father in heaven." Jesus died for the just and the unjust that He might bring us to God. (1Pet. 3:18) Jesus left the blueprint in the Bible, and I look to Jesus to see how He served others and pray to the Lord to give me a heart like His to draw people to Him.

As I continued to pray and seek God's heart, my relationship with Him became personal. He began to reveal Himself to me through His word, circumstances, and godly people. I began to really know the Lord as being faithful and full of grace and mercy. God showed me unconditional love and acceptance, which I needed the most at that time in my life, and I received it. The love and acceptance I have in Him is enough. He has touched my heart in such an amazing, powerful, but gentle way, and I want to live a holy life that brings Him glory (Gal. 3:13). I reflect on the prophet Isaiah, who says, "I will greatly rejoice in the Lord, My soul shall be joyful in my God; For he has clothed me with the garment of salvation, He has covered me with the robe of righteousness" (Isa. 61:10). I can rejoice in the Lord and be joyful! God has saved me and I'm totally covered by His robe of righteousness. Our righteousness is as filthy rags, but Jesus has made us righteous and it is a finished and perfect work (Isa. 64:6). I thank God that I am free and my eyes have been opened. My mind is renewed, and I have freedom as I continue to grow in the grace of the Lord (Eph. 2:8). I'm thankful to God that He showed me the only Way: Jesus. He already knew that we would never be able to live up to all the rules, so that is why He gave us His Son to die for all the sins of the world (Rom. 4:24). I thank God that I'm free from the guilt, shame, condemnation, depression, and feelings of defeat and hopelessness. I no longer seek to be accepted by people; I am accepted by God, and if people reject me for the sake of gospel, I'll just shake the dust off my feet and keep it moving. I have Jesus and in Him I have everything I need.

In the book of Acts, Paul and Barnabas face persecution at Antioch. The Jews oppose what the apostles are preaching. The Jews even drive them out of their region. What was Paul and Barnabas's reaction? They shake the dust from their feet and they are filled with joy and with the Holy Spirit (Acts 13:42–52)! The Thessalonians, though in much affliction, receive the word with joy of the Holy Spirit (1 Thess. 1:6). We may go through persecutions, rejection, or just difficult times in life, but we can be like the apostles and the Thessalonians and be filled with the Holy Spirit and joy. Joy is one of the fruits of the Spirit that we have when we live a divine life in Christ.

Abiding in the love of Jesus and doing what He commands us to do produces the fullness of joy.

> As the Father loved Me, I also have loved you; abide in My love. If you keep My commandments, you will abide in My love, just as I have kept My Father's commandments and abide in His love. These things I have spoken to you, so that your joy may be full. (John 15:9–11)

If we walk in obedience, we abide in His love. We can be sure that when we are in union with Christ, there will be no obstacle that we can't overcome, and through it all we can have a holy joy because we have faith that in the Holy God.

Prayer Matter

Father, in the name of Jesus, I thank you for the privilege of being able to ask in Your name that my joy may be full. I don't take this for granted, Lord. I thank You that You are sovereign, and You have all power in Your hands. In times when I am sorrowful, distraught, or discouraged, may I be mindful to look to You first. May going to You first become a like a "reflex" for me. I don't even have to think about it; I will run to You, my Refuge, my Rock, my Comforter. When I'm grieving, may I be reminded that Your Word says that You are close to the brokenhearted (Ps. 34:18). Release into me the oil of joy for mourning and the garment of praise for the spirit of heaviness (Isa. 61:3). Although sometimes I don't feel You close to me, I know that You are with me, and you will comfort me.

I release all discouragement, hopelessness, sadness, and sorrow to You. Give me a glimmer of hope, Lord, when I get tired, worn out, and want to give up. Give me a fresh perspective on my life so that I can see the blessings. Take away any hardness of heart, and help me to have a heart of gratitude for all You've done for me and from whence You have brought me from. Where I have been spoiled, unappreciative, and ungrateful, I ask You to forgive me. I don't want to disappoint You in any way.

Father, free me from guilt, condemnation, rejection, and shame. Create in me a clean heart, and restore to me the joy of my salvation. Uphold me by Your generous Spirit (Ps. 10, 12). Where I've been in bondage by false doctrine and ideas, I ask You to deliver me. Renew my mind according to Your Word, Lord. Where I have been rejected, I ask You to release Your healing balm upon me. May Your approval be enough to satisfy my innermost being. Take away all my need to be accepted by people. If I am accepted in by You, that is enough.

Shannon Bryant

I pray in humble confidence, knowing that in You my joy is complete, for you are my Joy. The joy I have in You doesn't fluctuate or change with my circumstances. My joy will remain firmly planted in my heart and spirit, and it won't go away. It's a steady flow of solace and bliss. With You, I have confidence that no matter the problem, I can position myself in Your loving arms for an abundant outpouring of Your joy. I have victory through Jesus Christ, and His joy will remain in me, and my joy will be full (John 15:11). Lord, release into me the spirit of joy, an unbroken joy, so that I can be strong to cope during the tough times and rejoice every day, no matter what the day may bring. I know You are with me and everything is going to work out for my good because I love You (Rom. 8:28). In Jesus's name, amen.

FIRM FAITH

Now faith is the substance of things hoped for, the evidence of things not seen.

—Hebrews 11:1

Something hoped for, evidence of things not seen, faith. Some people hope for husbands, homes, jobs, healing, or for loved ones to be saved. In the midst of desiring these things is the waiting period, and that's when we our faith is tested. When the results we want seem to take too long, can we keep the faith? Even though you can't see what you hoped and prayed for, can you still maintain your faith and believe God for it? Can you be positive that if it is God's will, it will be done? Can you persevere in prayer, expecting for what you are hoping for to come into fruition? Can you believe and expect the promises of God to be fulfilled no matter what the circumstances look like?

Right now, I am praying to God to help me to lose weight. Right now, when I look in the mirror, I have the unwanted extra weight, but I'm hoping for the weight to start coming off. I don't see it, but I sure am hoping and praying to God for it. I also have to take the necessary steps to lose the weight by eating right and exercising. I can have the faith to do it, but I also have to do the work. This requires me to make the decision to do the things that I need to do to lose weight and sticking to it. No matter how slow the process is, no matter what the scale says, or no matter how my body looks, I have to persevere and keep going by faith, knowing that if I keep pressing, I will see the evidence of what I have hoped for. Faith without the works is dead (James 2:17). So I have to put in the work to get the desired results that I need. My desired result is weight loss, which will lower my blood pressure and give me more energy. I'll sleep better, look better, and will hopefully prevent diabetes and many other diseases.

The Bible says, "The end of a thing is better than its beginning. The patient in spirit is better than the proud in spirit" (Eccles. 7:8). That's definitely true with exercise. In the beginning, it can be hard. You get out of breath quickly, and your muscles are sore. As you persevere and keep exercising consistently, it doesn't hurt as bad as it first did, and you build up endurance. Eating right can be difficult at the beginning, too. I love sweets, cookies, cakes, and chocolate. I have to give treats up if I want to reach my goal. Instead, I have to choose a better option, like a piece of fruit. My taste buds have to get used to healthier food: kale, hummus, and green smoothies. But after a while, I get used to it, and even start to like it. Eventually I start to feel better, and that encourages me to keep going. The key is to make a decision, commit to it, commit it to God, do things that you are in control over to nurture the thing hoped for, pray, and believe in God for it. If it is His will, it will be done: "Beloved, I pray that you may prosper in all things and be in health, just as your soul prospers" (3 John 2). Yes, better health is in my future. I can't see it now on the outside, but on the inside, my blood pressure is going down, and I feel a lot better. Just because you don't see things happening, does not mean God is not working on your behalf. He is all the while working it out, as my mother would say.

In the spirit realm, faith works in the same way. We hope and pray for something, and we can't see it with our eyes, but if we are in His will, and it's His will, we will receive what we ask for (1 John 5:14–15). Although we can't see it materialize, it's already there in the spirit. That thing hoped for, that seed, is implanted in your inner man. You nurture that seed with prayer, and you exercise your faith by believing. Next, you feed your faith by reading and meditating on the promises of God. Then, you trust God by resting and knowing what you hoped and prayed for will come into fruition. Just like I had to give up the sweets, you may have to give up something. You may struggle and have aches and pains along the way, but it will be more than well worth it when that promise hoped for is manifested. God is just good, not because we are good, but because He is more than faithful.

A real test of my faith came in 2013. I was suffering from severe insomnia, hypertension, and was diagnosed with a painful condition, which the doctors said had no cure. This also caused me to have really bad anxiety. Not only was I physically sick, I was an emotional wreck, and I felt like I was going to lose my mind. I was in severe emotional and physical pain for almost the entire year. A year may not seem long to some who suffer from chronic long-term illness, but for me—a person who had never been sick besides a cold or flu—it seemed like a very long time. My health was good up until then. Up until then, I ate what I wanted, drank whatever I wanted, and never gave any real thought to the damage I was doing to my body. Doctors could not help me, naturopath did not cure me, and the herbalist did not work. This made me more hopeless and discouraged, but I tried my best to keep my "mustard seed" faith (Matt. 17:20).

During this time, I prayed and cried out to God continuously, habitually, fervently, and desperately for healing. I wondered if God heard me. Sleepless nights would torture me, my heart racing and my blood pressure numbers elevated alarmingly high. My mind was never at rest. I felt like David in the Bible when he says, "I am weary with my groaning; All night I make my bed swim; I drench my couch with my tears" (Ps. 6:6). In addition to the sleepless nights, I was in pain the majority of the time. The condition that I was diagnosed with by my doctor had no known cure and to make matters worse, the medicine that doctor prescribed me for the illness with no cure, made me worse. Doesn't make sense right? There's no cure, but here's some medicine for you. I tried really hard not to get discouraged, but this was taking a toll on me, my marriage, and my family. I started losing a lot of weight and losing it rapidly—at one time at the rate of a pound a day. Although I could stand to lose the weight, I didn't want to lose it that way. During this time, I started to get really scared. I felt like my body had turned on me. I asked, "Lord, what is going on with my body? Take the pain away. Lord, I just want to sleep." I was thankful to God if I got two hours of sleep, but unfortunately, that was rare. I felt like I was going to lose my mind first, then my body would be next. I thought I was going to die.

Through it all, I still persevered in prayer. I begged God to make me better. My church prayed for me, my mom prayed for me, and my husband prayed for me in the midnight hour. I also had some powerful prayer warriors praying for me—those friends who you know can get prayers through to God. Even my daughter would come and lay in bed with me, pray me through, and encourage me in the Lord. Spending time in worship, laying prostrate, praying in the spirit, and praising and dancing before the Lord became a comfort for me. I was desperate for relief from all the pain I was enduring. I needed peace in my mind, and the only way I could get it was by being in the presence of the Lord. Getting in

God's presence would lift up my spirits, and although most days at first I didn't feel like praising, I pushed through the pain and did it anyway.

I remember starting to feel sorry for myself. Getting sick was during the time that I had really gotten serious about my relationship with God—no more playing around. I was on fire for the Lord. I read my Bible every day, prayed every day, attended church regularly, volunteered, witnessed, and was just busy going about my Father's business. I had finally gotten to my "happy place" when sickness struck me from out of nowhere. I remember thinking, "Why? Now I can't even do anything for the Lord; I'm in too much pain, and my body is not cooperating." I could barely leave my house any longer than a couple of hours just a few times a week. I wanted to feel sorry for myself. I mean I was just pitiful.

God revealed to me through my daughter that although I was sick, I could still be an effective witness to someone. I could still intercede for others and encourage others. This helped me to get my mind off of myself and helped me to focus more on being a blessing to someone. I began looking for opportunities to pray for others or to call and encourage someone, and this helped me so much. In fact, I know it was part of my own healing process.

Some days I would still feel really down, sick, discouraged, and ready to give up. I felt like God was not hearing my prayers. See, I was going to God for something. I was going to Him for healing, peace, and comfort. All my works were done for me to get the results that I wanted so much. In all of my asking, begging, and crying to God, He would give me something so precious, so indescribable. He gave me Him.

I began to speak God's Word over my body, read books on healing, and most importantly, I read the Bible. I read every healing scripture I could find in the Word of God. This was God's medicine, with no adverse side effects that you hear about on the television commercials: "If you are taking this medicine, it may cause headaches, nausea, drowsiness, suicidal thoughts, trouble breathing, stroke or even death." What? God's medicine was food for my spirit and healing for my body: "My son, give attention to my words; Incline your ear to my sayings. Do not let them depart from your eyes; Keep them in them in the midst of your heart; For they are life to those who find them, And health to all their flesh" (Prov. 4:20–22). For the record, conventional medicine can be and is beneficial, but for me during this time, nothing worked. It was God's will for me to completely trust in and depend on Him, the Great Physician, whom all healing comes from whichever way He sees fit to heal a person. There are many ways that God may want to heal. We must be sensitive to the Holy Spirit and His leading and use common sense, of course.

Eventually, my faith began to be uplifted! I not only spoke the Word, but by faith I started to believe the Word: "Faith comes by hearing and hearing the word of God" (Rom. 10:17). The more I started speaking and listening to Word of God, my faith became stronger! Though my healing did not come instantaneously and I could not feel it or see it, by faith I started to believe. Did I have doubtful days where I felt abandoned and couldn't take it anymore? Yes, but as time went on, the good days outnumbered the bad. I saturated myself with God's Word and spent time in His presence more and more. I believed but asked God to help my unbelief (Mark 9:24). My prayer even began to change. I prayed, "Lord, I pray for total and complete healing according to Your will, Lord. Even if I don't get healed on this side of heaven, help me to be of OK with that. Lord, help me to accept whatever Your will is for me." I didn't know what His will was, but I continued to pray for healing anyhow.

During this time one of my favorite scriptures to quote was Matthew 9:22, which reads, "But Jesus turned around, and when He saw me He said, 'Be of good cheer, daughter, your faith has made you well.' And I was made well that very hour." (emphasis is

Prayer Matters

mine) This passage really touched me; I felt like I had so much in common with the woman who suffers from an issue with her blood. Although her issue lasts for twelve years, and my issue was only for one year, it seemed a lot longer. The woman suffers many things from different physicians. Similarly, I went to several doctors with no results and still constant pain and sleepless nights. She spends all she has but still gets worse. In desperation, I also spent a lot of money and sometimes my last dollars for doctors, remedies, and prescriptions, with no relief. My persistent prayer was her prayer: "Lord if I could just touch the hem of Your garment (in the spirit realm) I know I will be made well" (Matt. 9:21).

Gradually, I was made well! Praise God! Jehovah Rapha, my Healer! Of course, I did have to take better care of myself. Dietary changes were necessary as were exercise, fresh air, and just really getting to know what worked for my body and what triggered my flares. Was this easy? No. It took partnering with the Holy Spirit to help me to make the changes I needed to make to get better. Trust me, I was so desperate that I did what I had to do. I was fed up with being sick. I'm still a work in progress as far as the eating right and exercise portions are concerned. But I'm not where I used to be. When I reflect on how sick I was, it motivates me to do better, and God blesses my efforts.

Prayers for healing are powerful, but we must work in accordance with our prayers. If we have faith, God has the promise, but we have to do our part: "Faith without works is dead" (James 2:17). I had the faith no matter how small it seemed at the time. But I also had to depend on God to give me discipline to eat better, exercise more, and reduce stress. Faith by itself, if it does not have the works, does not work.

This trial in my life helped me to grow spiritually, and I got to know God in ways I would had never known Him before. My mama couldn't help, though she tried. My husband did the best that he knew how, but he could not comfort me like God. I had close friends pray for me and encourage me, but in those times when I was alone, it was just me and God. In those dark times, nobody—I don't care how close they are to you—can keep you from being consumed like God Almighty. In that place of so much distress, turmoil, pain, and even doubt, He was always there. He never left me, and He never will leave me. His Presence is everlasting and a place of comfort like no other. Nothing can compare to His love and care.

Prior to my illness, I was very meticulous about keeping my home perfectly clean, beautiful, and immaculate. Now, keeping my house perfect is not all that important to me anymore. People can actually sit on my living room furniture now. It's not a "showroom" anymore—it can actually be lived in and enjoyed.

My daughter recently broke one of my candle holders that I'd loved so much. When it crashed to the floor and shattered in pieces, the look on her face was one of pure terror. To her surprise, I didn't say a word. I just continued fixing breakfast and told her, "That's OK; it's just a candle holder. It can be replaced." My daughter and my whole family looked in amazement. Now, that's progress. Going through that time of illness changed my whole perspective on life. Material things were not important to me anymore. God was most important, followed by my family and friends.

I used to be so busy that I could hardly sit down to have a conversation without wiping down the kitchen counters. As soon as I thought that my kids were finished drinking out of a cup, I would grab it quickly, then wash it in the sink. My daughters often tease me now when they are drinking a glass of water or juice and they sit it down on the counter. "Mom, I'm not finished with that yet. I'm still drinking it." It's funny to me now, but it's also sad in a way. I feel like I wasted so much time "doing" and trying to make a "perfect" life for my family that I didn't spend much quality time with them.

God brought a lot of good out of my seemingly bad situation: "And we know that all things work together for good to those who love God, to those who are called according to His purpose" (Rom. 8:28). Most importantly, I was able to draw close to Him and know Him personally in ways I could never have imagined. My life will never be the same. Secondly, I was able to draw close to family and nurture relationships. I no longer rushed out of conversations, and my mind wasn't thinking about what was next on my to-do list. Because when I was sick, I wasn't able to "do." I had to just "be." Now I take time to enjoy time with my family. Not only was this a time of spiritual renewal, but I also had time to slow down. I believe that God allowed it for the very purpose of strengthening my faith, and He showed me what was really important in life. He has to be priority above all else. He showed me the importance of taking care of my body, and I now appreciate my family more. God showed me His sovereignty, His trustworthiness, and His faithfulness. I now know Him as my Healer because He healed me. I know Him as my Comforter because at night when there was no one else to talk to, I talked to Him and He comforted me. I got to know Him well, and those sleepless nights were not wasted. I used those nights to talk to my Father. I know Him as my strength. When I felt like giving up, He strengthened me to keep going and renewed my bodily strength. Though this time of illness was the worst time in my life as far as my physical health, it was the best time for my spiritual health. I got to know God in a new and living way. If I had not had this time laying on back, looking up to God, I would never have had the experience of getting to know Him better. Not only did my family and I draw closer together, but this trial drew us all closer to God. It was all part of His plan.

Now, I have a better view. I see life from a more appreciative and grateful perspective. My heart is filled with gratitude for the things that I once took for granted like my health, family, and creation. I now take the time to smell the roses and observe creation in awe. Observing the beauty of the trees, its branches blowing in the wind like a perfectly orchestrated dance, was something new to me. I never paused to delight in creation. I began admiring nature, basking in the sun, soaking up all of God's goodness, and observing the birds of the air. All these things I had seen thousands of times before, but somehow it seemed like looking it at all for the first time. This caused a boost of faith, excitement, optimism, and thankfulness about life like never before. I knew God as the Creator and Provider and if He took care of all these things, how much more would He provide and care for me, His child? The flowers and trees were adorned so beautifully. He provided for the animals, and they didn't have to worry. They had to prepare, but He supplied. He causes the rain to fall from the sky, and He lights up the sky with the moon. He is omnipotent, omnipresent, and omniscient! He is the Creator of everything, and He is so strategic. We must live from faith to faith—faith at the beginning, end, and middle, every step in faith. Each time God brings us out of a situation, heals us, provides for us, protects us, and comforts is a faith builder. Every time God moves on our behalf, we build a stronger, more confident relationship with the One who is forever faithful. God has a plan. He has not forgotten you.

Prayer Matter

Father, in the name of Jesus, I thank You. You allowed a time of illness in my life to be a time of my faith being uplifted, a time of refreshment and restoration. At the same time, I got a revelation of Your faithfulness, and I know You as my Healer. This was also a time of being still and totally surrendering to Your will. I didn't know it then, but You were working out something in me so priceless. Like David says in Psalms 119:71, "It was good that I was afflicted, that I may know your statutes." Lord, I know that if I have even faith of a mustard seed, nothing will be impossible for me (Matt. 17:20). I put on my shield of faith to repel all doubt.

Father, create in me a hunger and thirst for more of Your Word, for faith comes by hearing and hearing the Word of God (Rom. 10:17). Enable me, Lord, to take better care of this body that You live in. Forgive me for not spending more time in fellowship with You and with my beautiful family. The time spent with my family is priceless, and I never want to take this time for granted anymore.

The time spent with You changed my life forever. I long for continual fellowship with You. Help me to walk intentionally moment by moment in Your Presence. I thank You that You allowed me to lie down. For in that lying down, my faith was lifted up. You are the Author of my Faith (Heb. 12:2). My Everlasting Father, I thank You that You didn't allow for me to give up. You knew just how much I could take. Lord, I was right there at the threshold of giving up. That's when Your love came in so powerful—but gentle—and flooded my heart with hope.

The flow of tears did not overflow and drown me in my spirit. The tears watered a place deep inside my spirit, and now I can produce more fruit for Your glory. A beautiful garden can grow now; the weeds are gone that were stunting my growth. Now I can plant seeds in others so that they can grow, too. Thank You for making a way of escape for me, and that way of escape is You. I know You are faithful and do just what You say, for I now know that the testing of my faith produces patience (James 1:3). In the midst of the waiting, You are completing Your perfect work in me, for my good and for Your glory. In Jesus' name, amen.

DIVINE GUIDANCE

Your word is a lamp to my feet and a light to my path.

—Psalms 119:105

Life is a journey with different paths to take. Knowing which path to take is confusing at times. We don't know whether to go left, right, stop, go, or stay. It can get puzzling at times, and you can get lost and frustrated. To illustrate, life with no direction is like me in my car before the invention of the global positioning system (GPS). Before GPS, I was a mess. I would get lost and would have to call my husband and ask him for directions, and he would send me in the right direction or get me back on the road I was supposed to be on. During that time of being lost, I would sometimes be afraid, unsure, anxious, confused, and frustrated. Life's journey is the same way when we are not sure what direction to take.

God has given us His "GNS" (God's navigational system), the Word of God. His Word is a lamp unto our feet and a light to

38

Prayer Matters

our paths, showing us the way to go (Ps. 119:105). If we follow His directions closely, we won't get lost. It may seem like we are lost sometimes, but if we follow Him and walk by faith, our destination is sure. We have to read the manual (Bible), study it, and follow it, and we will get right where God wants us to be. Reading the Word and partnering it with prayer is key in following the lead of the Holy Spirit. The Holy Spirit not only guides us into all truth, but He helps us to understand the Word of God also.

Sometimes we may think that we know where we are going. At times we are unsure if the direction we are taking is right. That's why it's imperative that we look into the Bible to see if where we are going is lining up with the Word of God. We must follow God's instructions in the Word. Sometimes there are bumps in the road, but He will smooth them out. The path may get crooked, but God will make it straight for us (Isa. 45:2).

At times we may want to go our own way, but this will only lead us on a dark path that leads eventually to destruction. Imagine you are driving on a route given to you by your GPS. It seems as if the GPS is taking you the long route so you decide to take a short cut. While driving you realize that you are really lost now. Before you know it you are approaching a side of a cliff, and you can't change course because your car is in front wheel-drive and rapidly approaching the edge. The same applies to following God's Word.

When we don't follow the God's Word, we get lost and before you know it you're headed into a danger zone and if you don't stop or God intervenes you could be headed for spiritual and natural death. Sometimes we try to take short cuts instead of going in the direction that God is leading us. Don't get me wrong there have been times when God's way has been faster, but most times God's wait is a slower pace with a bigger goal in mind.

Comparatively, when my dad cooks his famous chili it is a whole ordeal. He puts in all his special spices and ingredients and it has to simmer on low heat for the whole day. The aroma fills up the house and it smells so good. I often want to dig in before time but I wait with eager anticipation even though hours are passing, I endure. Besides, nobody is getting any until my dad says it time. It's finally done and I get a big bowl of the chili. I taste it and it's so savory, spicy and delicious. It was definitely worth the wait. Furthermore, if all the spices hadn't simmered and cooked in, it probably would not have created such a harmonious savory flavor. God's ingredients for us in times of waiting are patience, prayer, endurance, and faith. When we combine those ingredients they produce character in us and a hope in God that does not disappoint, in His timing. (Rom. 5:3-5) God's timing is most definitely worth the wait. The bible says the end of a thing is better than the beginning. (Ecc.7:8) God wants us to learn along the way and be patient. He builds up our character, endurance and uplifts our faith. When God says its time, He blesses us beyond what we could ever have imagined.

Waiting on God's time is crucial. I have gotten into bad relationships because I was impatient. Red flags were up everywhere but I followed my heart. Following your heart is a dangerous thing. The Bible tells us in Jeremiah 17:9, "The heart is deceitful above all things, and is desperately wicked." I followed my heart and ended up hurt, guilty, and ashamed. There is a blessing in obedience. We can save ourselves a lot of heartache if we just follow and stick with God.

We must follow the Leader, the Holy Spirit. The Holy Spirit is our Guide, the Spirit of the Living God. Isaiah 30:21 says, "Your ears shall hear a word behind you, saying, 'This is the way, walk in it,' whenever you turn to the right hand or whenever you turn to the left." We must pray and ask God to open our spiritual eyes and ears so that we can hear Him speak to us more clearly. Ask God for a sensitivity to the Holy Spirit's leading. The Holy Spirit leads and acts as our rear guard (Isa. 58:8). There is a great confidence in knowing He's in the front leading us and behind guarding us. We have to consciously choose to rely and obey the Holy Spirit for all of our decisions, moment by moment. This is called walking in the Spirit. "I say then: Walk in the Spirit, and you shall not fulfill the lust of the flesh." (Gal. 5:16) Walking in the Spirit is walking in obedience to the Word of God, following the Holy Spirit's promptings, and using godly wisdom—not going our own way, not us taking the lead, but step by step following our Guide (Gal. 5:16). The Spirit empowers us to live godly lives, and walking step-by-step by faith helps us not only to gain victory over sin but also gives us divine guidance.

The Holy Spirit can communicate to us through the Bible, a still small voice, a sermon, prayer, the preached word, people, godly discernment, and revelation. The key is to be sensitive the Holy Spirit's leading. The Holy Spirit-led life will not only guide you into all truths (John 16:13), but He will tell you what is to come, teach you what to say, nudge you in what not say, and will lead you in prayer. He will not only tell you where to go but also where not to go. These just describe Him as being our divine Guide. I addition, He is also our Helper, Comforter, Teacher, Standby, Strengthener, Counselor, Condemner of Sin, Intercessor, and Teacher. All of who He is guides us into the will of God and enables us to be led to walk in the Spirit.

God has a plan for your life and the Holy Spirit is your personal Guide. He's not only leading you, but He's inside of you (1 Cor. 3:16). If you have accepted Jesus Christ as your personal Lord and Savior, the very life of the True and Living God lives inside of you! Seek Him for direction in your life. The scripture in Proverbs 3:5–6 says, "Trust in the Lord with all your heart, and lean not on your own understanding; In all your ways acknowledge Him, and He will direct your paths." Oh, just trust Him with all of your heart. Follow Him more closely. Notice in the above scripture the word is "paths." God may lead you to do different things in different seasons. The key is staying close to Him, listening, abiding, obeying, praying, and worshipping Him. The road may get dark, but God will brighten your path. The further you go, the clearer your path will be, and you when you reach a place where you know God has led you, you can look back and see every mile marker that God placed to get you to His destination for you. Sometimes the way you are going may not make sense, but walk with faith in every step.

One example is the prophet Elisha. The things Elisha did didn't make sense but by his supernatural ability to believe God he released the power of God to do the miraculous. Elisha healed a spring of water by putting salt into it. Doesn't make a lot of sense to me, but the spring was healed by Elisha's act of faith. (2Kings 2:21-22) In another instance Elisha purifies a pot of stew. The stew was poisonous. So what was Elisha's solution? Flour, yes, Elisha put some flour into the pot and the stew was purified, served, eaten, and everybody was fine. Okay, flour to heal poisonous stew. Well there was nothing magical in the flour or in the salt that was put into the water, it was Elisha's faith in the living God! (2Kings 4:38-41)

Another awesome example of faith and the power of God is when a man that was born blind was healed by Jesus and received his sight. How did Jesus heal him? Jesus spat on the ground, made clay with saliva, and anointed the man's eyes. Jesus then told the man to go to and wash in the pool of Siloam. This man exercised his faith by being obedient and he was healed! (John 9:6-11) I tell you, sometimes things don't make sense and we can't figure it out or see where God is trying to take us. But be encouraged, trust Him, and allow Him to order your steps. Be obedient by faith and God will do wonderful things in your life. Your ability to believe God will release the power of God in your life and the lives of others that you may affect for His glory.

Acknowledge God, and get to know Him. The more you know Him, the closer you can walk with Him and depend on Him for every step. With the Holy Spirit as your Guide, you won't be lost. Now while traveling in the car, I don't get lost as much. I don't have to call my husband for directions anymore. The GPS does direct me to the long, scenic route sometimes to get me to my destination, but I just enjoy the ride and trust God that there is a reason for it. Just as in life, you may have gotten turned around a few times, run into a few detours, or even have taken the long, scenic route. You may have seen a lot of terrible things, but it won't go to waste. You will be able to help someone and tell them about what you saw and experienced along the way, and maybe they won't go that route. You can now tell others not to go this way or that way. You can help to turn others around and lead them in the right direction, toward God. God is so awesome! Our trips are never wasted if we turn around (repent) and start moving His way. He then will place others in our paths so that we might help them avoid pitfalls or help them to turn around and travel on the road that leads to eternal life. Going our own ways leads us off the path that God has planned for us, but if we stop, get into the word of God, heed His instructions, pray, and go the way He commands us to go, we will be positioned right where He wants us to be, in His will, the safest and securest place to be.

Prayer Matter

Father, in the precious name of Jesus, I give You glory for all of Your marvelous works. I surrender to Your guidance in my life. Lord, in times when I didn't obey you and went my own way, I thank You that You still kept Your arms around me. I thank You for mercy while I have traveled on my journey through life. You kept me from dangers that I saw, and I chose to keep going. You kept me from dangers that I could not see, and I am forever grateful. On my journey I fell into the pit many times. Thank You for always pulling me out, no matter how far down I fell. Enable me to avoid more pitfalls along the way by keeping my eyes on You and following You closely. Lord, give me a repentant heart, so if I ever get turned around or distracted, I will quickly turn back in Your direction and Your will for my life. Help me to walk in the Spirit moment by moment, from choice to choice, from decision to decision. May I never walk too fast and move ahead of You, moving so fast I miss the mile markers you have for me.

Help me not to move too slowly, missing what You have for me. May I stay in perfect pace with Your leading. I thank You, Lord, for when I was confused and frustrated, You turned me around and got me back on track. You never let me go too far, Lord. You pulled me back and pointed me in the right direction. You are the Good Shepherd (John 10:11). I allow You to continue to lead, groom, and guide me with Your Word. Refresh and pour out Your Holy Spirit upon me. Protect and guard me from all diversions from the enemy.

Holy Spirit, enable me to walk in the Spirit and not fulfill the lust of the flesh (Gal. 5:16). At times, my spirit is willing, but my flesh is weak. Help me always to watch and pray, lest I enter into temptation (Matt. 26:41). Open my spiritual eyes and ears so that I can hear You more clearly say "Go this way." Your command will lead me to the right destination. As I follow You, Lord, I ask You to give me discernment and revelation so that I will know when to stop, go, yield, or stay.

May I saturate myself in Your Word so that it will brighten my path. Release into me holy boldness to walk on the path that You have prepared for me. I don't have to be afraid or anxious. You are with me. You go before me and make my crooked places straight (Isa. 45:2). I pray that I will continue to walk into Your marvelous light and fulfill Your will and purpose for me for Your glory. Thank You, Father, for I don't have to be lost anymore. You have turned me around and placed me on the path to righteousness and the way that leads to the road of life eternal. Thank You for never giving up on me when I wanted to go my own way. I thank You for mercy that is from everlasting to everlasting (Ps. 103:17). In Jesus's name, amen.

HOPE IN GOD

*My soul, wait silently for God alone, for my expectation is
from Him. He only is my rock and my salvation; He is my
defense; I shall not be moved.*

—Psalms 62:5–6

How do you remain hopeful in devastating situations? Divorce
may be your reality right now. How can you get closure when
a marriage is supposed to last until death do you part? How do you
get over it and move on? The hurt and betrayal is unexplainable
and excruciating at times. Maybe the grief of losing a loved one has
you in a pit of despair and unimaginable hurt. You try your best to
pray and be strong, but you just can't seem to snap back. Could it
be that your child has gone off to college after your whole life used
to revolve around him and now the empty nest leaves you feeling
empty inside? Have you found yourself in an abusive relationship
and it is killing you inside and out? You may not have anywhere to

go or can't see your way out. Maybe you're struggling with an addiction you've tried so many times to break. You try your best to stop, but when hard times come, you go back to that old standby. You've lost your home due to foreclosure or unexpectedly unemployed. Your child, though you brought him up in the admonition of the Lord, he has gone astray and your prayers for him seem to be unanswered. Your parents are growing older into their senior years, and you are trying to balance your life with caregiving for them. It hurts to see them that way, but you have to keep pressing to care for them the best you can. Things just seem to happen, one thing after another, and you ask yourself, "What else can go wrong?" How do we keep ourselves from getting discouraged or frustrated? How can we be hopeful in a seemingly hopeless situation? Unfortunately, these are all common situations these days. But fortunately, God has supplied us with a hope: a hope in Him.

This hope in God is an optimistic expectation and assurance that God will bless your life in the future and give you endurance for what you are going through now. Hope is a constant expectation of something we can't see. We have the privilege to find a promise in the Bible and apply it to our circumstances. As children of God, we have confidence in knowing that God is working it out for our good, according to His purpose (Rom. 8:28). His purpose might be to build our faith and character or to draw us closer to Him. His purpose for allowing the "sufferings of this present time" (Rom. 8:18) leads us to fall at His feet with humble submission, surrendering all unto Him. His main purpose for allowing the test is to get us to conform to the image of Jesus Christ, which benefits us now and everlasting.

When I was a child, I hoped for many things. One Christmas, I hoped for one particular baby doll. This doll would mimic a real baby. The baby doll could be fed. You could give her water and even change her diaper. The legs and arms of the doll even moved to give the appearance of being a real baby. Oh, how I hoped for this doll all year long. I wanted her so badly. Did I think that I was going to get

Prayer Matters

her? I sure hoped I did. In fact, I was expecting her. My mom was not going to let me down. Early Christmas morning—I'm talking about two in the morning early—I got up and went under the Christmas tree to get my gift. This particular year, my brothers and I only got one gift each. And if I was only going to get one gift, I hoped it would be what I really wanted wrapped inside of the bright Santa wrapping paper. I nestled back in bed, and frantically, quietly, and carefully, I unwrapped my gift. There she was, the baby doll I had hoped for! Shortly after getting the doll unwrapped and taken out of the box, I realized the doll needed batteries. Oh, how I wanted to play with her right then, but I couldn't. I stayed up the rest of the morning with anticipation, waiting and waiting for daybreak. After what seemed like forever, I was able to get the batteries and place them in the doll. I was so excited when that baby doll started moving! She was activated! The excitement and joy I felt on that Christmas morning was incredible, and my hope was not disappointed!

People may disappoint, but hope in God does not disappoint (Rom. 5:5)! You may have hoped for something for a long time. You can't see it, but you hope and wait with expectancy. Full manifestation of what you hope for may take time. For example, when I got the much-anticipated baby doll, I was overjoyed. But when I realized I didn't have the batteries, I had to wait.

After I got the batteries and put them in the doll, the doll became activated. Our hope must be activated by our faith! Faith is knowing that God will work everything out for the good of those who love Him. But it's according to the power that works in us. The batteries placed in the doll gave the doll power to work. The hope placed in God gives us the power to activate our faith. When the full manifestation of what's hoped for comes, it brings joy, fulfillment, amazement, and most importantly, a heart of gratitude and thanks to God, our Father.

Moving forward in my life to my teen years, I pondered on what career choice I would pursue. I've always had a desire to help people. Although I didn't know or understand entirely what I wanted to do, I knew it would involve helping people. I narrowed it down to two things: a social worker or a nurse. I took a few nursing classes and did extremely well until I got to the clinical portion. When caregiving for the patients, I became very emotional. I couldn't take seeing people suffer. I resolved in my mind that I couldn't be a nurse. The thought of having a career where I had to witness the hurt and pain of others did not sit too well with me. So I set my hopes on becoming a social worker. I thought in my young mind that social work would not affect me as much as being a nurse. Reflecting back, I didn't understand it then, but I understand it now. Both take care of hurting people and are occupations that can tear at your heart, and in those careers what is most needed is a heart of compassion. I decided in my heart that I wanted to be a social worker and advocate for people who were in vulnerable and difficult situations. That was my plan.

Proverbs 19:21 says, "There are many plans in a man's heart, Nevertheless the Lord's counsel that will stand." I had hopes of going to college, getting a degree, and having a great career. After getting established in a career, I would get married and then have children. Well, let me tell you, my life did not go exactly in that order, and no, I am not a social worker. I ended up meeting a great man who is my husband of twenty-seven years. We dated for about three years, and then I got pregnant. We were married seven months after my daughter was born. This curtailed me going to college because now I was a mom and wife. I was able to be a stay-at-home mom for a couple of years. While I was enjoying being at home with my baby, there came a time when I had to work. I worked various jobs and finally settled down in the school system, taking college courses here and there. Meanwhile, we had another daughter. My husband and I had an awesome family, beautiful children, and a nice home. Somehow, my hope of becoming a social worker got lost between baby feedings, diaper changes, elementary school plays, helping with homework, girl scouts, high school, proms, taking the kids back and forth to college, not to mention paying for college tuition, and eventually a wedding. Wow! Where did all the time go?

Even though what I had hoped for did not come to fruition, I would not trade it for anything. God had a plan, and He was with me every step of the way. Even when I was a young, unwed mother, He was with me. Through all the guilt, shame, and rejection, He was with me, and He forgave me and helped me to forgive myself. Not only did He forgive me, but He restored me! He blessed me with a wonderful husband and beautiful daughters. God is marvelous, and His way is perfect. My hope is not disappointed! His plan was and is better than mine could ever be.

Sometimes things don't work out the way we'd hope they would. Some hopes and dreams don't manifest, or they don't manifest in the way that we would like for them to. Trust God, His plan, and His timing. God has unique plans for each of our lives. The details in my plan are unique to me. Yours is tailor-made by God just for you. Our hopes and expectations must be in God alone. Sure, we may get distracted by the cares of this world. But if we stay with God, He will bring us out victorious. We just have to be patient and yield to the will of God.

In trials it is only God who can deliver us out of our troubles. Our physical and emotional healing comes from God alone. He may use a doctor and medicine, but healing ultimately comes from Him. To help assist with emotional healing God may send someone to pray for you, talk with you, cry with you, but ultimately it is God who gives peace and comfort like no other. He may lead you to godly counsel, but He is the Counselor from whom all comfort comes from. He may use people as vehicles to carry out His plan, but it is ultimately He who brings us out.

During the hard times, press as best you can into His Word and into His presence. In these times, partner with the Holy Spirit, and this will help develop perseverance, which awakens our hope and gives us strength to go on. I encourage you to not give up! Hope in His Word and in His promises. Whatever the situation, find a promise in the Bible that applies to it. Meditate on the Word, pray the Word, and invite God into the situation through prayer. Unfortunately, some people are so discouraged that they can't pray or open the Bible. This is when you need someone to stand in the gap for you. Call a spirit-filled friend, someone who will not only pray with you, but be praying for you and encourage you in the Lord. Don't let the enemy get you to isolate yourself. One of the enemy's goals is to get you alone, hopeless, and depressed. This makes it easier for him to attack you because you are alone with no backup. Call for backup! Sometimes you need someone to tag team with you. Those times when you are depressed, tired, and ready to give up, call in reinforcement. Get a tag-team partner, a godly friend to intercede and encourage you, at those times when your load gets too heavy. Find someone who will pray down spiritual blessings from heavenly places on your behalf.

God can restore! "So I will restore to you the years that the locust has eaten" (Joel 2:25). He is your Refuge, your Strength; keep hope in Him. He has not abandoned you! You are not alone! If you are in Christ, He is in you! Abide and rest in Him. He is Immanuel, and God is with you! He has an awesome plan for your life! He is making and molding you, you are His workmanship, a masterpiece for His glory (Eph. 2:10)! He loves you, and He won't leave you alone to fend for yourself. If you are His child, you can be certain that you have the victory.

You will not only overcome for yourself, but you will overcome for others! The scripture says in Revelation 12:11, "And they overcame by the blood of the Lamb and by the word of their testimony, and they did not love their lives to the death." Our testimony is what God has done for us, and we are witnesses for Jesus. Telling others what God has done for us encourages others and helps them not to lose hope. Giving our testimonies can encourage us as well. It helps us to recall the faithfulness of God. So when we find ourselves in a position where our hope is diminishing, all we have to do is reflect on how He as has always kept His promises. Confess the goodness of the Lord and the power in His word.

So as the Spirit leads, tell others where God has brought you from and what He has done for you. Nothing is wasted. Nothing you went through will be wasted when you pour it back into others. Don't give up: "For I know the thoughts that I think toward you, says the Lord, thoughts of peace and not of evil, to give you a future and a hope" (Jer. 29:11). In all humbleness and faith, trust God and thank God in everything.

Prayer Matter

Lord, I thank you for Your gift of hope, which I receive by faith. I thank You because I can live a life anticipating Your goodness and faithfulness. Father, be the lifter of my head in times of disappointments. I invite You into every situation that seems unworkable. Give me rest in my mind and spirit while I allow You to work the situation out in Your good timing. Bring me to a place of absolute assurance and trust. Even though the situation may look unfavorable, I know that You are always advocating for me, and I can be optimistic about my future.

Don't let bitterness, resentment, and anger overtake me. I ask You, Lord, to take away these negative emotions and let the mind of Christ arise in me. Touch my heart and heal all the shattered places. I pray that I will be whole in You. In those times when You are silent, give me strength to hold and to go deeper in Your Word. Endow me with endurance to pray more fervently, and seek You in Your divine presence.

I know that You are working out something far greater in me that I can't understand right now. Although I can't grasp it now, I trust You, Lord. Open my heart and mind to receive all that You have for me while I'm waiting for Your promises to be fulfilled in my life. Give me patience and

Shannon Bryant

endurance so that my hope will remain active and continual without doubt, fear, and worry. You alone are trustworthy; people have let me down and broken promises, but I know that You are the Promise Keeper.

You are able to do more than I can ask or think according to the power that works in me (Eph. 3:20). May the hope of the power in me, which is You, be activated by faith and be manifested in all areas of my life. Father, help me not to labor in my own strength. Laboring in my own strength only wears me out and brings discouragement and frustration. I know I can do all things through You who strengthens me. (Phil. 4:13) Help me to mature in faith so that my roots will grow deeper in You. Even in the midst of trials I rejoice in You Lord.

I know this world and its desires are passing away, but I know that I have a greater hope in glory that is eternal. All else is preparation to get me to that glorious destination. I wait for You with an assured, expectant heart, knowing that hope in You never fails. In Jesus's name I pray, amen.

PRAYER LIFE

Then He spoke a parable to them, that men always ought
to pray and not lose heart.

—Luke 18:1

Jesus spoke a parable about the widow and the judge. I've always loved this parable, specifically the persistence of the widow. She keeps troubling the judge for justice from her adversary. The judge resists awhile, but he eventually gives in because the widow troubles him continually and wearies him. The judge in this parable is insensitive to people and doesn't fear God, yet because of the widow's persistence, he answers her and gets justice for her from her adversary. How much more will God Almighty do for us when we persevere in prayer! We cannot weary Him enough in prayer. In fact, we are to pray without ceasing (1 Thess. 5:17)! We have the most glorious privilege to go to God anytime, anywhere, and bring requests, supplications, and thanksgiving to our heavenly Father.

Whatever the need, it is found in Him. If we don't ask, we don't get. Sure, He knows what we need before we ask, but He wants to spend time with us. He wants us to get to know Him and develop relationships with Him to heighten our faith. Our lives must be lives of communing and communicating with Him, establishing continual fellowship with Him. Our lives and the lives of others consist and depend on prayer. Prayer is the lifeline that connects us to our Lord, who hears, answers, and bestows blessings from heaven to earth for us and to others we may intercede for. When we pray, He answers.

If prayer is so crucial to our lives and to the lives of others, why do so many people struggle with praying? Time is an issue for some. We live in a busy, fast-paced world, with schedules filled to capacity, and finding time to pray can be difficult. Some struggle with prayer because they think that they can't pray properly, or they just don't know what to say or how to pray. Others may think that God does not hear them when they pray. They are filled with so much condemnation, guilt, and shame that they feel like they can't go to Him in prayer.

Whatever the reason, it is crucial—a matter of life and death—that you have a consistent, powerful prayer life. Your life and the lives of others depend on you going humbly before God, for His will to be done on earth as it is in heaven for His glory. For you to live a victorious, abundant life, you must have victorious, abundant prayer.

Jesus gives us an awesome example of a strong prayer life. He is in constant fellowship with His Father in prayer. In fact, He gets up early to pray. Luke 1:35, says, "Now in the morning, having risen a long while before daylight, He went out and departed to a solitary place; and there He prayed." Jesus makes it a point to get up early and seek God in a private, solitary place. If time is an issue for prayer, then maybe you can consider following Jesus's example. No matter how busy your schedule may get, making a prayer appointment with God is possible and extremely important.

Prayer Matters

We have all kinds of appointments we make in life, like hair appointments with our beauticians. Some would never miss a hair appointment. Without our hair being styled and those grays covered up, we may feel incomplete and unattractive. Then there are those gym appointments. We can't miss those because our bodies have to be tight and right. Me, I have no problem missing a workout, but there are some people who are very committed to going to the gym. Lastly, what about that doctor's appointment? We have to see doctors when we're sick, when we need to get checkups, or maybe when we need to get a prescription filled. It's good to see a doctor regularly for the prevention of diseases and illness, not just when we're sick. This is the same with God. When we have a problem should not be the only time we go to God. Although we can go to God anytime, why wait until there is a problem or something going on to go to Him? In fact, when we go to God regularly, we can prevent many of the complications that may occur in our lives. Just as doctors give us instructions on how to eat, incorporate lifestyle changes, and take prescriptions, in prayer we get directions, guidance, and God's remedy for life. Going to God in prayer is an appointment that we cannot miss, and it must be made a priority in order to have a healthy, abundant life.

Personally, I find spending time with God in the morning is best for me. Like how some people have to have that cup of coffee first thing in the morning to get them going, I have to spend time with God in prayer first thing in the morning to get my day started right. If I happen to miss my prayer time, my day just doesn't seem to go right. It's like I can't function well, like that coffee drinker who doesn't have their cup of brew. I have to have that time. See, only God knows what the day may bring, and spending intimate time with Him in prayer gives me strength and endurance to make it with a better attitude. I find I have more peace and joy throughout the day when I have divine communion with the Lord. Daily prayer also helps when I run into challenges during my day. There will be challenges, but prayer helps me to better endure them and gives me direction as to how to deal with them.

God hears us at any time, day or night, and we can go to Him freely. Pray throughout the day, in the car, while walking at the park, or in your neighborhood. Pray all the time, anytime, just make time to do it. Some people may work different shifts, and they may have to find a time more conducive to their schedules to pray. Jesus also spent the night praying to God (Luke 6:12). Others may find it better to pray once theirs kids are off to school or after their spouses have gone to work. Time invested in prayer gives back an invaluable, priceless return, spiritual riches in heavenly places, and empowers us to live victorious lives now.

We must yield ourselves fully unto Him in His glorious presence. During this time of fellowship, we partake of His holiness. All that we need is poured out to us from Him. We may be in need of healing, deliverance, peace, financial need, or joy. Whatever the need, it's ours for the asking and His pleasure to bless us with it. If our Lord and Savior Jesus Christ needs time alone with Him, how much more do we need to take the time out to seek His face, not just for things, but for who He is and to give Him praise and thanks?

Feeling inadequate in prayer is also a hindrance to people spending time in prayer. Some feel like they don't know how to pray or what to pray. Praying is simply pouring out your heart to God, your heart to His heart, communicating with Him about what's really on your heart, what you are feeling, and what you have need of. Prayer is giving thanks. There are many types of prayer such as intercession, worship, praise, thanksgiving, petitions, and supplications. Although it may seem difficult, it is simple. Prayer is a desire to know God in a more intimate way; it's a two-sided conversation. Don't feel like you have to do all the talking; take time to be still and listen for His voice. There is no need for special, eloquent words. Speak sincerely to your Father. He loves and cares for you, and He is truly concerned about your feelings, needs, and circumstances. He knows, and He understands, listens, and answers. We can come boldly before the throne of grace with confidence that we can receive grace in time of need (Heb. 4:16). There is no need to feel inadequate before our Loving Father.

As a child I was a labeled "daddy's girl," and some say I still am. Whenever I called my dad, he would come. If I was upset about something, no matter the time, he would be on his way. Daddy to the rescue! When he arrived, I would feel secure, safe, and comforted. We'd often talk about whatever the problem was. As I reflect back, I can't even remember some of those problems. They seemed major at the time, and I was a very emotional little girl. But no matter how small the issues were, my dad showed genuine interest and concern. He listened, gave me advice, and assured me that everything would be OK and that he would be there for me when I needed him. Comparatively, our Heavenly Father is on His throne, waiting for us to call on Him. No problem is too small or too big. He is available anytime and anywhere. He's there, longing to listen you. He is patient, kind, and loving. He will wrap you in His loving arms and let you know that everything is going to be all right. God will give you direction, guidance, and comfort. He is always there when you need Him. Come as you are with a sincere heart. No fancy words are needed, just simply come.

Partnering with the Holy Spirit will also teach you how to pray and assist you with what to pray for. We don't have to labor in our own strength; the Helper will help us to pray. He will enlighten our spiritual eyes and teach us to pray. In Romans 8:26, Paul speaks about our inability to pray: "Likewise the Spirit also helps in our weaknesses. For we do not know what we should pray for as we ought, but the Spirit makes intercession." Pray before you pray. Ask the Holy Spirit to lead you in prayer and to pray through you. The Holy Spirit will give you discernment and revelation on what to pray for and who to pray for. Praying the Word of God, His will, by the power of the Holy Spirit, is the most blessed, powerful prayer. His Word does not return void; pray the Word of God (Isa. 55:11).

There have been times in life when I've struggled with prayer. Most of those times were when I was bound in sin. The things that I had done, which I knew were wrong in the eyes of God, had caused me to be ashamed to go before Him. I couldn't go boldly with confidence before Him because I was condemned. The sins I so badly wanted to stop doing, I kept doing, and I was ashamed. The prayers I prayed that I falsely believed to be repentant prayers were not really repentant prayers. Yes, I was sorry and ashamed, but I was not repentant. I wasn't godly sorry. If I was really repentant, I would've turned completely away from the sins that had so easily entangled me. I didn't feel worthy or good enough. This was right where Satan wanted me to be. Every time I fell into condemnation, I wanted to give up. That's what the enemy wants; he wants you to be in a state of hopelessness so that you won't even try anymore. He wants you to think that you can't conquer the things that have you bound. It's a dangerous cycle. You try to live right in your own strength. Then you fail because you are striving in your strength. Next, the condemnation consumes and torments you and you want to quit.

This horrible, familiar cycle always achieved the same result for me. I struggled in prayer, I felt defeated and unworthy. I fell into condemnation. The Holy Spirit will convict us of sin but what He does not do is condemn. (John 16:8) Condemnation is from the enemy, it is a dreadful heaviness and torment that makes you feel like there is no hope for you. Condemnation leads to despair and sorrow. We might also have feelings of giving up and thinking that we won't ever be able to change. Condemnation keeps the focus on you, instead of keeping your eyes on the Lord.

God's conviction makes us want to change and brings us to repentance. Conviction doesn't look at the sin but looks to Jesus for deliverance and help to overcome. God's conviction is truly a blessing and I

Prayer Matters

thank Him for always keeping me aware of my sin. And boy does God keep me aware when I'm doing wrong. To tell you the truth, there are times when I say, in my flesh of course, "God is not letting me get away with nothing." Those nudges of knowing that I'm totally out of line can be overwhelming at times. But I thank God for it, there's no telling where I would be without God redirecting, and disciplining me. I thank Him for His grace and I continue to grow in it. I don't have to be so much as sin conscious, but God conscious.

Jesus bore all of our sins, guilt, shame, and rejection on the cross, so there is no need to feel condemned. In 1 John 3:20–21, it says, "For if our heart does not condemn us, God is greater than our heart, and knows all things. Beloved, if our heart does not condemn us, we have confidence toward God. And whatever we ask we receive of Him."

It is imperative that we forgive others if we want our prayers answered. In Mark 11:24–25, it says,

And whenever you stand praying, if you have anything against anyone, forgive him that your Father in heaven may also forgive you your trespasses. But if you do not forgive, neither will your Father in heaven forgive your trespasses.

Forgiveness is a prerequisite for answered prayer. We waste our time in prayer if we have bitterness in our hearts. I'll use a heart as an example. The heart is the vital organ in the body from which all life flows. When an artery in the heart is blocked and is hardened, it blocks the flow of blood to the heart muscle. This is what causes health problems such as strokes or heart attacks. Prayer is the vital organ from which our spiritual life flows. When we hold bitterness in our hearts, it hardens our hearts and blocks the flow of our prayers from reaching God. Not forgiving others is detrimental to our spiritual and physical health. Forgiving those who have hurt us is hard to do

Shannon Bryant

at times. We must do it for ourselves by faith. By faith we can resolve in our hearts to forgive. Forgiveness is often a process that takes time. Ask God to help you by faith to forgive, and He will. When we are free of bitterness, we are free of a heavy weight, and we can know that our prayers are able to flow freely to reach heaven. Furthermore, if we want forgiveness from God, we have to forgive others (Matt. 6:14).

The Bible says in 1 John 1:9, "If we confess our sins, He is faithful and just to forgive us our sins and to cleanse us from all unrighteousness." If we confess our sins before God, He will forgive us. And as a heavenly bonus, He will cleanse us of all unrighteousness! God knew every sin we would commit, and He still sent His only begotten Son to die for us. If we were to never sin, there would not had been a need for God to send His Son to redeem us. The key is to try to live lives that are pleasing to God through the power of the Holy Spirit. Will we mess up? Yes. Can we come to God with sincere, repentant hearts and ask for forgiveness? Absolutely! Is He pleased with sin? No. But if we confess our sins to God and ask Him for forgiveness, He does forgive us. Sometimes the problem is that we have a difficult time forgiving ourselves.

Trust that God has forgiven you, forgive yourself, and move forward into the newness of life: "There is therefore no condemnation to those who are in Christ Jesus, who do not walk according to the flesh, but according to the Spirit" (Rom. 8:1). If we are in Christ Jesus, there is no condemnation. Thus, we have access to go boldly, freely, with confidence before the throne of God!

Praise God for the victory! Worship Him with a sincere heart of gratitude. Ask in faith!

But let him ask in faith, with no doubting, for he who doubts is like a wave of the sea driven and tossed by the wind. For let not that man suppose that he will receive anything from the Lord; he is a double-minded man, unstable in the Lord. (James 1:6–8)

It is a blessed privilege to be able to go to God in prayer. We don't need a priest like in the Old Testament. Jesus came and tore the veil from top to bottom, and now we can go freely to Him (Matt. 27:51). Rejoice in the Lord! Persevere in prayer! Don't give up! If you don't know what to pray, open your Bible and pray the Word of God, the most sufficient prayer. When in trials, make Him your first option, your first "go-to" Person. May you live to pray and commune with your Father. Run to throne of grace not only for yourself but for others as well. As you seek Him in prayer, time after time you will be tremendously blessed in ways you never imagined.

Prayer Matter

Father, God, I thank you for hearing and answering my prayers. I thank You that whatever I ask in Your name, You will do, and Jesus may be glorified (John 14:13). Lord, when I feel inadequate, when I feel like I'm not good enough, or when I feel condemned, help me to recognize those for what they are: lies from the enemy. Help me to refuse to let those thoughts and feelings enter my mind and spirit. Pour out Your Spirit of forgiveness to me so that I can forgive those who have hurt me. Lord, I ask that You help me to do it by faith. At times, I don't want to forgive people who have hurt me because I'm still hurting from the things perpetuated against me. I ask You to help me by faith to release all bitterness, resentment, and anger I have toward anyone. Cleanse me from all of these negative emotions because they are only hurting me. I release bitterness to You, Lord. I don't want anything hindering me from having a continual flow of fellowship with You. Free me from the burden of the hurt that was perpetuated against me. I ask You to heal and close every open wound. May I be healed and made whole in every broken area, even in areas that I don't even know are dismembered. Bring healing.

I thank You, Jesus, for bearing all my shame, guilt, and rejection on the cross. I thank You for tearing the curtain so that I may go freely to the throne of grace, not only in my time of need, but anytime. Lord, when my life is so hectic and it seems like I can't find time for You, help me to find a space in my day for You and me, alone. May I set and keep my appointment with You, Lord. It is an appointment that I cannot afford to miss. It's in Your Presence that I not only receive from You but that I have the sacred opportunity to give You glory and worship You in the beauty of Your holiness.

I stand at the foot of Your throne, asking You to teach me how to pray the effectual, fervent prayer of the righteous that avails much (James 5:16). Open my eyes to discern the sacred spirit of prayer. Give me a strong desire to pray for others. Anoint and equip me for intercession. Enlarge my understanding of how to pray for others. Lord, I know that it's not all about me but what you want to do in me and through me for You and for Your glory. When I give all to You, I receive all from You, according to Your will. May Your will be done in my life, on earth, as it is in heaven (Matt. 6:10). In Jesus's name I pray, amen.

PATHWAY TO FREEDOM

Then Jesus said to those Jews who believed Him, "If you abide in My word, you are My disciples indeed. And you shall know the truth, and the truth shall make you free."

—John 8:31

Jesus gives us a clear path to freedom and assures us that if we abide in His word, we will know the truth, and the truth will make us free! He further emphasizes this promise in John 8:36. He says, "Therefore, if the Son makes you free, you shall be free indeed." When we know His truths, abide in Him and His Word, then we shall be made free. It sounds like a clear path, a road with easy clear directions. If the map is so easy to read, then why is it so hard to follow the directions? There may also be pits, booby traps, pot holes, and decoys along the way. Either we are lured by Satan to take routes that were not intended for us, or we just want to go our own way. If we are not careful, we can become slaves to sin, and the enemy will gladly be our slave master. Ending up in bondage, all tied up and bound is a terrible state to be in, I know. Unfortunately, this road is a road often traveled. I've been down this road a few times myself. Thank God that He has provided us a pathway to freedom, where we no longer have to be enslaved anymore. Jesus is the Way, the Truth and the Life (John 14:6). Let's go.

First, we see in this scripture that the Jews whom Jesus was talking to believed Him. We must believe Jesus and trust Him to do and complete His work in us. Then, Jesus says to abide in His Word. We must read the Word, receive the Word, and demonstrate the Word continually. Jesus Himself is the Living Word. Abide in Him and rest in Him. In Christ your strength will be perfected. Abiding in the gospel of Jesus Christ in the Word of God will show you the truth and the way.

God's Word washes and cleanses us from sin. This is a continual process. When we are wise to respond to God's Word and allow it to cleanse us, we will be made like new. We will be cleansed, sanctified, and washed. Our filthy garments will become clean and fresh as He clothes us with His righteousness. As we abide in His Word, it saturates our spirits with His holiness, and we become holy. His Word will become established in us, and He will help us to turn our eyes away from worthless things and revive us according to His way (Ps. 119:37).

When we abide in His Word, the Word reveals the truth: Under the divine guidance of the Holy Spirit, biblical truths will be revealed to us. He will enlighten our spiritual eyes of understanding and teach us all things. The Holy Spirit will teach, interpret, and bring clear understanding and revelation to the Word and things of God. Scripture will start to come alive. Passages that you may have read before will have new meaning. The truth will be revealed, and as you receive and obey the truth continually, you will be made free.

Prayer Matters

This takes a desperate dependence on the power of the Holy Spirit. It's a moment-by-moment decision to walk in the Spirit and not fulfill the lusts of the flesh (Gal. 5:16). There are going to be times when urges and temptations may seem to overwhelm you, but God has made a way of escape.

> No temptation has overtaken you except such as is common to man; but God is faithful, who will not allow you to be tempted beyond what you are able, but with the temptation will also make the way of escape, that you may be able to bear it. (1 Cor. 10:13)

As I stated earlier my struggle with alcohol had been a vicious cycle for years. My first drink was given to me at the age of fourteen by a close family member. Further on in my teenage years, I gradually started drinking more and also started smoking cigarettes and marijuana. At nineteen I got pregnant with my first daughter. By the time I was twenty, I had gotten married to my daughter's father, and we started a good life together. My marriage was pretty good, and I had no major problems. My children were well-balanced and thriving. I made sure that they did their homework and chores. I took them to rehearsals and activities. My house was immaculate. I went to work and accomplished all of my wifely and motherly responsibilities. Despite my weekends of partying, most Sundays my family and I made it to the house of the Lord. Oh, I can remember so many Sundays going to church with hangovers. The beat of the drums, clapping, and loud singing made my head feel like it was about to explode into pieces. From the outside looking in, you would think that we had almost a picture-perfect life.

But in real life, I had inner turmoil. I suffered from bouts of depression, anxiety, and insecurity. So in order to feel better—to feel secure, confident, and to mask pain—I drank, and I drank a lot. Alcohol became a Band-Aid to cover up all of my emotional wounds. A Band-Aid only covers up; it does not heal the wound. Although it seems to protect and cover up the wound at the time, if the wound does not get exposed to air, it will not heal. An emotional wound works the same way. If it doesn't get exposed, it will get worse, and like an infectious disease, it will spread to different areas of your life. The temporary comfort that alcohol gave me would only get worse over the years. The Band-Aid needed to be taken off and exposed so that my emotional wounds could heal.

Although I was very functional, my drinking had gotten progressively out of control. I had my periods of sobriety but never anything lasting. My life began to be a blur of weekend binges and weekday burdens. I had let God down again. Mondays were the day when I would start my new beginning. Meaning that, starting Monday I was going to live my life right. Trust me I've seen years of Mondays before I could finally get free. But I had good intentions. I was going to stop drinking and really live my life for God. I mean, I was really going to do it this time; until the weekend came again. Every week was a sequel to the week before with the same old tired ending.

Although I didn't drink during the week, I had convinced myself that because I only drank on weekends, I didn't have a problem. But the problem was not when or the days I would drink, it was the amount that I would drink. I reflect on how much I alcohol I consumed on a weekend, and I thank God that I'm still here. I would try to cut down, but a little always turned into a lot. I was so empty on the inside and though I had everything I ever wanted in life, I wasn't happy. I didn't have the joy of the Lord on the inside of me. Sure, my husband and kids made me happy. They were my life, and in them was all my happiness found. Not until I sought the Lord and let Him take His rightful place on the throne of my heart did I have joy and that joy became my strength to be free.

Once I sought God for real, my life began to change. I surrendered every part of my life to Him the best I knew how: by faith. When problems would arise, instead of going to vodka, I went to Him. I had to intentionally with the help of the Holy Spirt strengthening me make the choice to go to God. The amazing thing about God is that when you go to Him in desperation, crying out sincerely for help to overcome, He helps in a way that transforms your life. He draws you by His Spirit, and you start to long to be in His Presence, and it is then that transformation begins to take place. It almost feels effortless. While you adore Him, He is transforming you. While you give Him your best, in exchange He adorns You with peace like an ever-flowing stream, so pure and full of the Living Water that hydrates, refreshes, and fills all the empty places in your heart. Those secret places of hurt and pain that no one knows about but you and Him, He heals with His gentle but mighty healing hand. When you seek God with all of your heart and soul, you will find Him. When you find Him, you will never be the same; you will be set free.

It can't be just another emotional experience. I had so many emotional experiences of crying at the altar, sobbing, and begging. Although my intentions were good, deep down I had not surrendered all. I hadn't gotten really tired and fed up with the drinking. I thought that I had laid my all at the altar, but I hadn't. If I had, I wouldn't have ended up in the same wretched place again, a place I thought that I would never be, more depressed, defeated, and ashamed than I was before. My wounds needed to be healed for my freedom to come.

If emotional wounds are open and need healing, they need to be exposed. Don't keep them inside. First, pray, and seek God. He heals like nobody's business: "He heals the brokenhearted and binds up their wounds" (Ps. 147:3). Be still and allow God to bind up your wounds and heal those hurt and shattered places. He is faithful to do it; He is the salve, the healing Balm bringing miraculous healing everlasting. Some wounds are deep and need more attention, for example, the hurt, shame, and guilt of being molested as a child by a family member or someone trusted to be around you. In this case, it's beneficial to have a trusted friend, pastor, or even a counselor to talk to; this furthers the healing process. Be prayerful and use godly wisdom. Sometimes it's a huge burden just carrying all the hurt inside, and once you let it out and tell somebody, you may begin to feel relief. It's not your fault. Be free from that lie today! It's not for you to take ownership of it. You didn't inflict the pain; the pain was inflicted on you. The good news is that God will completely heal you. No more guilt, no more shame; you are free in Jesus's name! You don't have to allow what happened to you in the past to affect your future happiness. God will do it for you. He did it for me.

Once you are free, never go back to what God has delivered you from. It is very dangerous territory to return to something that had you bound. God has given me a special scripture that I often have to reflect and meditate on. It is a reminder to me to not go back to my old habits. It is found in Galatians 5:1: "Stand fast therefore in the liberty by which Christ has made us free, and do not be entangled again with a yoke of bondage."

When God has delivered you from something, don't go back to it! I am a witness that if you do go back, the desire for whatever it is will be stronger and it will be harder for you to be free again. Luke 11:24–26 says,

> When an unclean spirit goes out of a man, he goes through dry places, seeking rest; and finding none, he says, 'I will return to my house from which I came.' And when he comes, he finds it swept and put in order. Then he goes and takes with him seven other spirits more wicked than himself, and they enter and dwell there; and the last state of that man is worse than the first.

Prayer Matters

Our spiritual house should be so filled with the Holy Spirit and the Word of God that the unclean spirit will not have room to come back and dwell again. Each time I relapsed into drinking, the struggle to stop got more difficult each time. During the latter time, I felt like it was almost impossible. That is because the unclean spirit will try to come back and bring spirits more wicked than himself, but if we are filled with the Holy Spirit and the Word of God, then the unclean spirit will not get inside. So please, whatever God has set you free from, don't entangle yourself with it again. You will only set yourself up for a stronger battle. Secure your spiritual house with the best security spiritual house system, Jesus. Look to God immediately when tempted. He gives the sufficient grace and power to endure temptation. When tempted, pray, read the Bible, submit to God, resist the devil, and the devil will flee from you (James 4:7). Make the decision that you want to be free, for real. Submit to God, and be committed to stick with your decision no matter what. It takes a made-up mind, and God will help you every step of the way. It comes to the point of asking yourself, "How badly do I want to be free?" You have to love God more than whatever has you bound. As strong as my desire was to drink, my desire to be free had to be just as strong and stronger.

Finally, an essential part of the freedom process—often the hardest part—is forgiveness of those who punctured you with emotional wounds. Although it is difficult to do, to say the least, it is imperative for healing.

Healing will not take place if you don't forgive. Forgiveness is for your overall emotional, spiritual, and physical well-being. When we don't forgive, it can hurt us in so many areas. Our relationships can suffer, our health can suffer, and our overall well-being and quality of life are affected. Furthermore, God does not want us to carry bitterness around. Just like excess body weight, it weighs you down and is not good for your health. Emotional baggage weighs you down, and it's bad for your emotional, spiritual, and physical health. When we carry too much of it, we are not free to live the lives that God has purposed for us. We are not built for it. Our jobs are to cast our cares on Him, and He will care for us (1 Pet. 5:7). We have to make a decision to forgive. It is a process; it may not happen instantly. You may not feel like it, but you are only hurting yourself and others around you if you don't. Forgive by faith. Ask God to help you to forgive the person who wronged you, and He will enable you to do it, but you have to be willing. Forgiveness is for you and not the perpetrator. Forgiveness will free you up, take a huge load off of you, and allow your life journey to be more pleasant and enjoyable because you don't have to carry the extra weight of bitterness anymore. When you forgive, that person has no power over you anymore and no more control over your life.

"Now the Lord is the Spirit; and where the Spirit of the Lord is, there is liberty" (2 Cor. 3:17). The Spirit gives us freedom! Chains broken, shackles loosed, unnecessary weight dissolved, wounds healed, hurt removed, addiction extinct, fear vanished, guilt expunged, shame eliminated, and whatever it is that holds you in bondage—annihilated! You are free to be all you were created to be, in Christ's image, for your good and His glory.

Prayer Matter

Father, I come to You in Jesus's name, thanking you for freedom! Whom the Son sets free is free indeed! (John 8:36) Thank You, Jesus, for bearing my freedom on the cross. I don't have to be weighed down by guilt, shame, condemnation, bondage, and sin. Lord, You paid the price for it all. All I have to do is believe in You and abide in Your word, and You will help me to know the truth, and the truth shall make me free.

Lord, I know that I can't break free in my own strength. I have tried so many times in my own strength and thought that I was free awhile, only to end up going back to the thing that had me bound. I know that only You can bring change in me that will last. I ask You for strength to help me to endure when temptation arises. You alone are faithful, and You will not allow me to be tempted beyond what I am able to bear. Help me to recognize and take the way of escape that You have provided for me (1 Cor. 10:13).

Thank You, for there is no place too far that I have strayed that You cannot reach out Your boundless hand and pull me back from. No matter how tied up I am in sin, I can be loosened. I stand still to allow You to bind up my wounds so that I can be healed and made whole. I thank You because there is no place so dark and gritty that Your light cannot shine and bring freedom. I thank You for pulling me out darkness into Your glorious light. I can see now! My eyes can see through the murk and gloom. You are the light of the world and when I follow You, I will not walk in darkness. I have the light of life (John 8:12)!

Where I have been imprisoned in my mind, I ask that You would help me bring every thought into captivity to the obedience of Christ (2 Cor. 10:5). Deliver me from all past devastating memories and hurts, and enable me to move forward into the future that You have planned for me. I don't want to be imprisoned by my past anymore, so by faith I surrender to the "new thing" that You are doing in me and through me (Isa. 43:19).

Release into me a spirit of rest, peace, and freedom. I know that there is no peace for the wicked (Isa. 48:22). Enable me to continue take Your yoke upon me so that I can find rest for my soul (Matt. 11:29). Father, I thank You for coming to set the captives free (Luke 4:18)! I'm no longer bound. You are my Deliverer, my Strength, and my Refuge. In Your presence is where I long to be; there my freedom lies, my liberty. Thank You for setting me free. Yes, I'm free indeed. In Jesus's name, amen.

GOD WILL SUPPLY

And my God shall supply all your need according to His riches in glory by Christ Jesus.

—Philippians 4:19

In today's society there is so much uncertainty. The economic state of our world is in chaos. Stock market fluctuations, government shut downs, unemployment, high food prices, high taxes, and the cutting of much needed services can set the environment for panic, frustration, fear, and worry. Often the pressures of life can get overwhelming. Where do the underprivileged senior citizens go for help to pay their utility bills when the program to assist senior citizens doesn't exist anymore? What does the single parent do when the program to subsidize her childcare is no more? She desires to work, but now she can't afford to pay childcare and meet other monthly expenses at the same time. How about the widow who can't make

Prayer Matters

ends meet and is forced to leave her home? Then there is the person who is caregiving for his or her aging parent because the agency that helped to provide care is now nonexistent. The young person who is fresh out of college and full of ambition can't find a decent job, and on top of that, he or she has a ton of student loan debt. The husband and wife are working one and sometimes two jobs, but still the threat of foreclosure is real. These and many more situations are what an alarming number of people face every day. To say it can be overwhelming is an understatement. We can be encouraged that if we are in Christ, we have the privilege and the hope of God's promise to supply our needs. *Jehovah-Jireh*, translated, "The Lord Will Provide," has promised to supply all of our needs.

In Matthew 6:25–34, Jesus gives us perspective on how we are to view our needs being met. We don't have to worry. He gives us assurance that God will supply all of our needs. In verses 25–27 He says,

> Therefore, I say to you, do not worry about your life, what you will eat or what you will drink; nor about your body, what you will put on. Is not life more than food and the body more than clothing? Look at the birds of the air, for they neither sow nor reap nor gather into barns; yet your heavenly Father feeds them. Are you not more of value than they? Which of you by worrying can add one cubit to his stature?

I know it sounds good, but yet we are still human, and worry can set in. It really comes down to asking yourself, "Do I really trust God? Do I really trust that He will supply food, clothing, shelter, peace, and joy?" It's really a matter of trust. If we really trust God to do what He says, then we shouldn't worry.

I was a chronic worrier for most of my life. I mean lingering, persistent worry. I would always be worrying about something or someone. Then, when the issue I was worrying about was resolved, I'd find another situation or person to worry about. It sounds crazy, but that was me—caught in a vicious cycle of worry. At times, I still struggle, but it's not nearly as much as I used to. I'm learning to trust God more fully with every situation, spouse, child, bill, health, etc. Worry does not add to your life; it subtracts. It takes away health, peace, joy, and it's a waste of time: "Cast all your cares on Him for He cares for you" (1 Pet. 5:7). Once you give your cares to God, don't take them back by worrying. Do all you can do to work in accordance with your prayer, but don't take on the burden of worrying. Give your worry to God and say, "Lord, this problem or person is yours now. I give it to You. I trust you to work it out for my good and for your glory." Leave it there, let God do His work, and be at rest.

I often look at the deer family that comes in my backyard from time to time. I think of how God provides for them. Although they have to put forth effort and go out to look for food and water, God provides. I've never seen a malnourished one. In fact, they look strong, healthy, vibrant, and quick. I love watching them out of my window as they graze through the grass. I look at them and think to myself, "I know if God takes care of them, how much more will He take care of me and my family? We are his children." In fact, just as the deer expect to find food, we too should have the same expectancy from God for our needs. Matthew 6:26 says, "Look at the birds of the air, they neither sow nor reap nor gather into barns; yet your heavenly father feeds them." What an assurance we should have in our heart that God will take care of His own.

God knows all that we need, and He delights in supplying our needs if they are according to His will. The key is to seek first His kingdom and His righteousness (Matt. 6:33). We have to make seeking the kingdom of God and His righteousness our first priorities. We can't let the cares of this world distract us from the things of God. We must strive to live holy lives in obedience to Him, which glorifies Him. A big part of God being glorified through us is sharing the gospel with others and being lights to others. I always try to

Prayer Matters

keep the mind-set that all that God gives to me, I will give to others. Reading the Bible, praying, studying, and even my trials are preparing me to help somebody. God promised that when we put Him and His righteousness first, all these things shall be added unto us. It will be His way and His exact time, but we can be assured that if we seek first His kingdom and His righteousness, we will have our needs met. It's a sure thing: "But those who seek the Lord shall not lack any good thing" (Ps. 34:10).

Romans 8:28 says, "And we know that all things work together for good to those who love God, to those who are called according to His purpose." Your idea of good may not be God's idea of good, so always keep this in mind. Your idea of good may be a new car. God's idea of good may be for you to keep the car you have because He knows that you really can't afford the new car at the time. God knows that having the new car will add to the financial struggles you already have and in turn put pressure on your already delicate marriage. My good idea may be for me to move to another state. God's good may be for me to stay where I am because my aging parents are here, and they could really use my help. In being a blessing to my parents, I'm being blessed with such precious moments with them. If I had moved, those memories would have turned into regrets. In both of these scenarios, it does work out for the best. God knows what's best for us. He is all seeing and all knowing. It works together for good according to His purpose, not ours. His purpose is for us to be conformed to the image of His Son (Rom. 8:29). One thing that I am sure of is that He is Sovereign, and I have to trust that whichever way He works it out, it's perfect and its part of His plan for my life.

As I reflect back on my life, He has kept me from some major mistakes. These are things that I thought were good but could have been devastating or even life-threatening. Looking back, I see that God has remained constantly, faithfully supplying my every need. This encourages me whenever I doubt God. I reflect back on how he healed. He healed my father twice from cancer and he's been in remission for seven years. I think about times when money was short and a bill got paid somehow. God saved my brother from a horrible motorcycle accident, which the doctors said my brother wouldn't live from after having little to no brain activity. My brother is alive and well, and although he is in a wheelchair, he is cognitive and has taken steps! I could go on and on about God's goodness of the Lord. Looking back on the goodness of the Lord and His faithfulness encourages me to look forward in faith.

Even what seem to us as disappointments are really just God's way of getting us where He wants us to be, like the job opportunities that I could never seem to get. I'd go to interview after interview, and a couple of the jobs I was just about guaranteed never offered me positions. I never got the call backs. I was so distraught and felt like a failure. Why could I never get the job of my dreams? I even went back to school and still never could even get my foot in the door of a company. I was very disappointed at the time, but I now know that those jobs were not part of God's plan for me at that time. If so, He would've opened a door of opportunity for me to have those jobs. He had a plan, and those jobs were not part of it. These disappointments, which seemed to me at the time like steps backward, were actually steps forward into the future that God had planned for me.

In hindsight, I can see God's faithfulness in so many situations. When in doubt, I remind myself of all that He's brought me from and brought me through. His goodness is purposeful, glorious, for my good, and for His glory. Whenever you are in doubt, I encourage you to take the time out and look back. Think on the things that could've gone for badly for you that God turned around for your good and worked out in your favor. There are times when He moves on your behalf in such a marvelous way, even in situations that seem hopeless. God provides every time. It may not be the way that we would expect or prefer, but He does. He is more than faithful, and He is able to provide above all that we can ask for or think of (Eph. 3:20).

If you are in Christ, and Christ is in you, you have the assurance that He will not forsake you. You are not left alone in times of need: "He who did not spare His own Son, but delivered Him up for us all, how shall He not with Him also freely give us all things?" (Rom. 9:32). God so graciously gave His Son, His only begotten Son, for us. To give such a precious gift to us is an expression of His love for us. That is how much He loves us. Just to think and ponder on the magnitude of the love He has for us to give His Son is inconceivable and yet remarkable. If He gave such a precious, priceless, perfect gift to us, how much more will He provide for our earthly needs? He gave freely His Son, and He gives freely to us. He gives in His timing, working out something in us. I often ask myself in troublesome times, "Lord what do you want me to learn from this?"

God allows adversity, trials, and tribulations (AT&T) to produce perseverance, character, and hope in us (Rom. 5:3–4). This in turn builds our faith. It gives us optimism about the future, no matter how uncertain or dim it may look. We tend to look short term; God looks long term, with a more eternal view. He is working out a greater purpose in us that we don't yet understand. But as we reflect back, we can often see God's hand in our lives, working things out His way for specific purposes. Maybe we are needing financial blessings, but in waiting for the blessings, we are learning to be good stewards over what God has already provided and learning that we can live on less than what we thought we could. It could be that sickness is allowed by God for the purpose of getting us to value and appreciate our bodies, thus provoking us to take better care of ourselves. This is not always the case but I believe in every trial there is something that God wants us to learn so that we can continue to grow. If we don't grow we're stagnant and that keeps us stuck in the same place. God is trying to get us where He wants us to be. God's main purpose is to get us to the place where we are transformed into His image. (2 Cor. 3:18)

Perhaps the devastation of divorce is weighing heavily on you. You not only feel rejected, neglected, and betrayed, but now you have to bear a financial burden. The kids need you, and you try to be strong for them, but you are barely strong enough for yourself. God wants to fill every void. He wants to bestow on us all our earthly needs, but most importantly, He wants to bless us with spiritual blessings (Eph. 3:1): the gift of eternal life through Jesus, the Word of God, justification, hope, joy, peace, sanctification, redemption, wisdom, and many other blessings. In Matthew 6:10, Jesus says, "Your will be done on earth as it is in heaven." In heaven and in Christ are these spiritual blessings, and unlike earthly blessings that satisfy and provide for us temporarily, spiritual blessings are for now and eternity.

The Bible tells us in Hebrews 10:36, "For you have need of endurance, so that after you have done the will of God, you may receive the promise." By doing the will of God, we align ourselves up to be blessed with the promises of God. He promised to never leave us or forsake us (Deut. 31:8).

He will go before you, be with you, and never leave you. So you don't have to be afraid, worried, or discouraged about Him meeting your needs. He promised that He would do it! Have faith, believe, trust, and align yourself with His Word. By doing His will, you will have what you need in Him and through Him. Don't forsake the promise by giving up.

All the promises of God in Him are Yes, and in Him Amen, to the glory of God through us.

—2 Corinthians 1:20

Prayer Matter

Father, I come to You in the name of Jesus. I thank You for loving me so much that You freely gave Your Son. I cannot comprehend Your great love, Lord, but I'm so thankful for it. Lord, I confess that in times when I'm going through a difficult situation, I get doubtful and afraid sometimes. In times when I am in need of endurance, help me not to get weary, for I know I will reap if I faint not (Gal. 6:9). I ask You to forgive me, Lord. Enable me to rely on and receive Your sufficient grace. Your strength is made perfect in my weakness. I thank You that when I am weak, I can come to You, and I'm never alone. You are here to help me to continue to stand (2 Cor. 12:9).

By seeking first Your kingdom and Your righteousness, I know I will have all that I need (Matt. 6:33). There is no need to worry or to be anxious. You are my Father; You will take care of me. Father, I commit all my cares to You. I ask that You give me peace and a spirit of expectancy. While I'm waiting, I will praise You, Lord, for I know the promise that is on the way. I know that You will supply every spiritual, emotional, and physical blessing. I am Your child, and you provide for Your children.

Lord, may I walk upright so that no good thing will be withheld from me. Lord, you see where I have need. Lord, I ask you to pour out a blessing. I pray against all tendency to worry. Give me patience while waiting with expectancy. May I never be stagnant in waiting. I will actively seek You, Lord, and Your will for my life.

You loved me enough to give Your Son. I know you love me enough to give me everything that I need. Lord, it's my heart's desire for it never to be about me and my needs all the time. May I often ask You, "What do you want to do through me, for others? How can I be a blessing?" Give me Your heart, God's heart for people, so that the love You give me I can give back to others. I know it is more blessed to give than to receive (Acts 20:35). The blessing is in the giving. In Jesus name, amen.

GODLY WISDOM

*If any of you lacks wisdom, let him ask of God, who gives
to all liberally and without reproach, and it will be given
to him.*

—James 1:5

Reflecting back on my life thus far, there are more times than I
care to remember when I have not used godly wisdom. Some
decisions I've made were based on my own fleshly desires, or I just
made decisions based on the wisdom of this world. Thinking back,
some decisions that I made I really felt in my heart were the right
things to do at the time but turned out to be the wrong things.
The decisions we make in our lives lay the foundations for the way
our lives will go. We can either use the wisdom of the world, which
is foolishness in God's sight (1 Cor. 3:19) or we can use godly wisdom. The Bible says that if we lack wisdom, all we have to do is ask
God for it, and He will give it to us liberally. He will abundantly

give us His wisdom to make decisions based upon His word, which equips us to live a life not only pleasing to Him, but godly wisdom will also help us to avoid a lot of unnecessary life complications.

"Wisdom is the principal thing; Therefore, get wisdom" (Prov. 4:7). Wisdom is invaluable and foremost for us to get true understanding, discipline, and direction in our lives from our Heavenly Father, who with wisdom founded the earth (Prov. 3:19). One of my favorite scriptures in Proverbs 8:35, which says, "For whoever finds me [wisdom] finds life, and obtains favor from the Lord." Both verses encourage us to get wisdom and find wisdom. To find something, we have to look for it. Where do we look for godly wisdom? The answer is from above, a heavenly wisdom that can only be found in God, in the Word of God, and communicating with God.

The Bible says in James 3:17 that, "The wisdom that is from above is first pure, then peaceable, gentle, willing to yield, full of mercy, and good fruits, without partiality and without hypocrisy." First, godly wisdom is pure. Pure is without contamination. Pureness is nothing that will spoil, poison, or contaminate you. For example, pride, envy, anger, selfishness, gossip, bitterness, and resentment are contaminants to our spiritual lives.

The pureness of godly wisdom is untainted by the world and its lusts. It's consecrated, divine, and righteous. A pure substance has a constant compilation or makeup of the sample. The wisdom from above comes from God that is pure and contains the constant makeup and attributes of God. He is pure, holy, true, and perfect.

Consider how arsenic, chemicals, and bacteria are some things that contaminate water and make the water unclean and dangerous. Some of the effects of contaminated water are nausea, vomiting, and cramps, or even death, just to name a few. These effects are detrimental to our health so pure uncontaminated water is needed for hydration and for our bodies to function well. When pure wisdom from above is not applied in our lives, there are also bad effects. Some of the effects are shame, guilt, condemnation, strife, resentment, bitterness, and lives filled with grief and discouragement. Not choosing pure wisdom damages our spiritual health and can do harm to our physical health as well. If we are in poor spiritual health, our emotional lives can suffer. This causes stress not only in our minds but in our bodies too, and then we can develop hypertension, ulcers, stress headaches, and many other stress-related illnesses, which could possibly lead to death. Pure wisdom keeps us from being defiled by the world and its lusts. If something is contaminated, the value of it is lessened. Wickedness and choosing to go our own ways lessen our quality of life. God has a plan for our lives, and it's not for evil but for good, to give us a future and a hope (Jer. 29:11). God has a good plan, and using godly wisdom will enable you to live it out.

Secondly, wisdom from above is peaceable. Obedience is necessary to have peace. The Bible tells us that there is no peace for the wicked (Isa. 48:22). In those times when I was habitually practicing sin, I had no peace at all. The Holy Spirt would convict me every time, and I'm so thankful. I never felt comfortable in sin, so I always desired somewhere deep inside that I didn't want to live that way anymore. In God's will, there is a peace that surpasses all understanding, and that alone makes me determined to never go back to the way I used to be.

As a teenager, I made a lot of bad choices. The teen years are years filled with insecurity and peer pressure. You're just really trying to find your way and learn who you are. At the same time, you want to fit in and be liked by your peers. By the time I was a junior in high school, I was at my third high school because my family had moved around a lot. I was reluctant and afraid about attending yet another school. Furthermore, I had to start over making new friends. This was a challenge for me because I was quite shy. But eventually I started to meet new friends. After a while, I began to get into the party scene. It started out with just alcohol, then escalated to marijuana. On almost a daily basis I was getting "high" on my way to school, sometimes during school, and often after school. In my mind, I thought this would help me overcome me being timid. Thinking back, I think that I was also covering up a lot of emotional pain from my childhood. And most importantly, I wanted to fit in and be "cool." I thought I was fun to be around and popular with the "cool" crowd, and I was enjoying it. This was a trap that the enemy had set for me, and I had walked right into it.

The wisdom from above is also gentle and willing to yield. When I think of gentle, I think of mildness, softness, peace, meekness, and humility. These characteristics seem fragile, but they are actually characteristics of great strength and discipline. I find this willing-to-yield wisdom from above is quite useful in marriage. I love my husband from the deepest depths of my heart, but—and I know you married people can attest to this—there are going to be times when you have to use godly wisdom and yield. You have to figuratively put up that yellow traffic sign in your brain and mouth and yield. Yielding before having to stop is navigating carefully. This takes a lot of discipline and practice.

Don't worry; in marriage you will get a lot of practice. And after over twenty-six years, I have not quite mastered it yet, but I'm a lot better at it than I used to be. There have been many times when I'd have to pray, "Lord, help me not to say what I want to say. Lord, put a guard over the door of my mouth. Lord, I know I'm right about this and he is wrong. I really have to get this off my chest. Lord, it wants to come out so bad, I want to say it so bad." Then, *bam!* The words that I was trying so hard not say come out of my mouth like shooting fire! As soon as I say them, in my mind I'm saying to myself, "I knew I shouldn't have said that." Now I have to deal with a full-blown disagreement that could have been avoided if I had just yielded and waited until my emotions were not so high. Bad timing can turn a small issue into a heated argument. It takes godly wisdom, self-control, and humility to take a step back and wait until a better time to have a discussion. Pray, count, take a

Shannon Bryant

deep breath, put your hand over your mouth—do whatever it takes to avoid bickering. Believe me, it's not about having the last word or being right. It's about pursuing peace and showing love and mutual respect for each other.

The word of God tells us in the book of James 1:19–20, "So then, my beloved brethren, let every man be swift to hear, slow to speak, slow to wrath, for the wrath of man does not produce the righteousness of God." In difficult circumstances and confrontations, how do you react? It's difficult, especially in the workplace. It seems that no matter the career path you take, there are always people there to test you. You try your best to hold your tongue and hold back dirty looks. You pray for them, and they seem to get worse. You pray for yourself and ask God to help you, but what you really want to do is tell them off and get it off your chest in a not-so-nice way. Responding with gentle wisdom is not what your flesh wants to do.

I believe God allows for us to go through these times of testing because He wants to see what we are really made of. Can you really be an example of His love when you want to curse somebody out? I encourage you, no matter how hard it gets, to stand on the word of God and pray for those who persecute you. Praying for those who persecute you is using gentle wisdom versus doing what your flesh wants to do. God will give you the strength to yield. If you humble yourself before the Lord, He will exalt you (James 1:10). Believe me, I know it takes more strength to be gentle and not return evil for evil. It takes more strength to love those who persecute you and even more strength to bless and pray for them (Matt. 5:44). Are you going to feel like doing it? Most likely, no. Is it what God says for us to do? Yes. We have to do it by faith and trust God that it's all a part of His plan to complete His work in us and through us. There are times when we have to speak up, be prayerful and ask God to give you wisdom in timing, give you the words and the tone. These are times when God has to truly intervene. Lord help us.

Prayer Matters

Next, wisdom from above is full of mercy. I thank God for extended mercy on my life. Every day I thank Him for His mercy. It's a good thing that His mercy endures forever, because that is the extent to which I need His mercy in my life. Because we fall short, we are in need of His mercy. We don't deserve it, but God extends His mercy to us. God has compassion for us, and His compassions are new every morning (Lam. 3:23). Imagine that every morning when you wake up. Can we extend that same merciful, godly wisdom, showing compassion to others every new morning? Can we wake up in the morning, having a clean slate with everyone, and not harbor bitterness against anyone? Especially people who might have misused you, talked about you, or have done you wrong in some way?

Jesus shows the ultimate act of mercy when He came down from heaven and walked this earth in the flesh. He literally put Himself in fleshy, human skin. There is nothing that we have been through or are going to go through that He cannot relate to. He felt all the things that we feel, and He endured temptations (Heb. 2:18). He felt every emotion, persecution, rejection, and ridicule. Yet, He showed an immeasurable amount of mercy and compassion by dying for our sins and giving us the gift of everlasting life. We have the same power we just have to utilize it to show Christlike mercy towards others.

Finally, the wisdom from above produces good fruits without partiality and without hypocrisy. It produces the fruits of the Holy Spirit: love, joy, peace, patience, kindness, goodness, faithfulness and self-control. A tree is known by its fruit. Jesus is the Vine and if we abide Him, we will produce good fruit (John 15:4–5). Allow Him to nourish you. May He rain on you with His everlasting flow of the Living Water of the Holy Spirit, which produces life-giving, good, pleasing, and satisfying fruits. This fruit is without partiality, wavering, or double mindedness. His fruit never spoils or goes bad like the fruit of the world. Its taste is always sweet and not bitter like the fruit of this dying world. The fruit of the world is filled with worms like; envy, jealousy, hate, deception and fleshly desires. The results are a life filled with temporary pleasure, shame, and resentment, and this fruit will leave a terrible taste in your mouth. The fruit that comes from godly wisdom is without hypocrisy. It's not deceptive or insincere. It is trustworthy, genuine, ripe, and good.

When we get wisdom from above, we are able to live victorious and successful lives. Most importantly, we live lives that give glory to God. Wisdom preserves us, protects us, guides us, and give us favor from the Lord: "Length of days is in her right hand, in her left hand riches and honor. Her ways are ways of pleasantness, and all her paths are peace. She is a tree of life to those who take hold of her, and happy are all who retain her" (Prov. 3:16–18). Yes, she (wisdom) is a tree of life, but we must take hold of her and retain her. Take hold of the tree of life by faith. In the Vine you will have everything you need to live a life that glorifies God and to produce fruit for His kingdom.

Prayer Matter

Father, in the name of Jesus, I thank You for wisdom from above. I thank You, Father, for watching over me and keeping me when I didn't know You and Your infinite wisdom. You say in Your Word that if I ask, You will give me wisdom liberally (James 1:5). Lord, I need Your wisdom all the days of my life. Without You, I am lost, not knowing where to go or what to do. I invite You to be involved in every decision I make. I don't want to be out of Your will, Lord. I will seek You, for in You is where wisdom is found. I will search for it like a precious treasure. Crown my head with wisdom and incline my heart to understanding and knowledge, not as the world gives, but as You give life-giving power to me.

Give me discernment and revelation to see the trap set from Satan before I step into it. Shield me, Lord, from every plan of deception that the enemy has plotted against me. Show me where there are areas of my life that are out of Your order. Father, help me to prioritize according to Your Word. Also, show me the areas in my life where things need to be eliminated, and give me the strength to get rid of them.

I pray that You will give me clarity of mind, free of all confusion, disorder, and chaos, so that I can hear Your instructions clearly. Wisdom is the principal thing, and it is imperative for victorious living (Prov. 4:7). May my closest associations be with the wise. Help me not to walk in the way of the ungodly so that I may be blessed (Ps. 1:1). May my house be built with wisdom, and by understanding let it be established (Prov. 24:3). Make me the wise woman who builds her house. I don't want to be the woman who pulls her house down with her own hands (Prov. 14:2).

Give me keen spiritual eyesight so that I can follow You more closely. Only You can see what's ahead. Give me your godly wisdom so that I am always aligned with Your will and purpose. I don't want to learn things the hard way. I've done that before, and it was horrible, frustrating, and derailed me from Your plan for my life.

Lord, may I be mindful to always consult You and seek You in prayer and in Your Word regarding my every decision. You are my Life Coach, and Your plan for my life is good. Guide my every step by Your infinite wisdom from above. In Jesus's name I pray, amen.

MOVING FORWARD

*Brethren, I do not count myself to have apprehended; but
one thing I do, forgetting those things which are behind
and reaching forward to those things which are ahead.*

— Philippians 3:13

Reflecting on past events, experiences, and feelings can encourage you, bring you joy, and give you motivation. However,
reflecting back on your past can also bring feelings of guilt, shame,
rejection, condemnation, and regret. It all depends on where you
allow your mind to go. Paul first encourages the believers in the
above scripture to forget those things which are behind. Now this
is coming from Paul, formerly named Saul of Tarsus. Saul is a per-
secutor of Christians and the church of God. Saul is present when
Stephen, a martyr, is stoned to death by the Sanhedrin. After ston-
ing Stephen to death, the Sanhedrin lay their clothes at the feet of
Saul (Acts 7:57–58). Acts 8:1 says, "Now Saul was consenting to his

death." Acts 8:3 says, "As for Saul, he made havoc of the church, entering every house, and dragging off men and women, committing them to prison." Now, Saul causes chaos and wrecks the church, then he then arrests the believers and locks them up. Furthermore, he consents to the murder of Stephen, a follower of Jesus. Let me tell you, if Paul can forget those things which were behind him, so can you and I. Whenever my mind tends to wander back to negative things that I've done in the past or bad experiences, I think of the Apostle Paul. It encourages me that no matter what you have done, if you accept Christ as Your Savior, repent, and ask forgiveness, it does not matter. Your sins are forgiven and you are able to start over again with a clean slate, a new beginning. You can start over like you have never sinned. How great is that?

In contrast, it doesn't have to be you who brings up the unfavorable things in your past; it can be others—yes, your friends, associates, and even family. When you give your life to Christ and start to really live for Him, people will remind you of who you were and what you used to do. It can be hurtful. Those reminders can make you feel kind of down. You try so hard but you can't seem to live it down. God has turned your life around, and now you have to hear these shameful things from others. People identify you by what you used to do, or who you used to be. They may not know or understand that there has been a change in your heart and mind. You are now living for Christ, not for the approval of people.

I thank God that He can take a habit away from you and you won't even desire it anymore like alcohol or cigarettes. When I stopped smoking cigarettes, it was difficult for me to be around people who smoked. I would smell the menthol and watch people as they puffed their cigarettes, inhaling and exhaling with such great satisfaction. I could just taste the menthol. It made me want a cigarette so badly. I just couldn't be around it. Now, I can't stand the smell of it. How could I have ever inhaled that horrible-smelling, cancer-causing, toxic, chemical-containing smoke into my lungs? I got to the point that the thrill was gone, and I didn't even miss it, whatever "it" may be. Your desire to please God has to be stronger than your desire for "it" and your desire to please people and feel accepted by them. Once Jesus is Lord over your life, you are not defined by your past anymore (2 Cor. 5:17). Your identity is in Him.

So how do you deal with the "bringer uppers"? I was the type of person who would not say anything. Keyword "was." I would feel hurt, of course, because I've always been the type of person who cared a lot about what people thought of me. I'd probably whine to my husband about it, and he would tell me what I should have said. My feelings were hurt very easily. Being a follower of Christ definitely requires tough skin. Christ's followers in the Bible suffer much persecution, for example, the Apostle Paul. But he took pleasure in sufferings and persecutions for Christ's sake (2 Cor. 12:10). I've always had a special admiration for the Apostle Paul. He was totally and completely sold out for God, and boy did he have a past.

We all have pasts, but we have to leave the past in the past. When people bring it up, you can just say, "Thank God I'm not that way anymore. God has brought me a long way!" This can easily turn into a great opportunity to tell them about how God has changed your life. A good friend of mine told me once, "The word of God is either going to draw or drive." It's either going to draw them to Christ or drive them away. When you attempt to share your testimony with others, they can either desire to hear more about how God delivered you, or they may choose to change the subject. If they choose to change the subject, you probably won't have to worry about them bringing it up again. In fact, I have seen many rooms empty and people scatter when a bold Christian arrives. As time goes on, people will stop bringing up your past. They will see the change in you. If you continually live a life that brings God glory, then they will take notice and respect that. You see, how we live our lives is our greatest, most powerful witness to those we encounter.

People will hold you to your past, but don't you dare hold yourself to it! Forgive yourself, and keep walking by faith. Don't look back.

Some past hurts can hold such a strong grip on us. There are some things we bring on ourselves and some things that happen to us that we have no control over. Some people may have been molested by a close relative or family friend in the past. This was a person they trusted and loved, but they ended up violating their victim and subjected them to horrible things. The shame and emotional scars are hard to forget and recover from. A person may be violently raped by a stranger. Memories haunt you, even when you sleep. The betrayal of a spouse who has an affair can be hard to move forward from. The marriage abruptly ends after twenty years. It was supposed to last forever. What do I do? Where do I go from here? The fatherless son has to be the man of the house because his father abandoned him and his siblings. He often looks out the window in anticipation, waiting for Daddy to come back. He knows deep down inside that his father is never coming back, but he always hopes that he will show up one day. Many suffer from abandonment issues as a result of being given up by a parent. Think of the loss of a loved one. Your heart aches with pain, and tears soak your pillow. The pain is so hard to bear. When will it ever end? A woman in her midlife is patiently waiting for God to send her husband. She has remained pure and has been faithful in serving Lord. She wonders when will her husband come? There are many disappointments in life. How do you find strength to keep going with optimism and hope?

Times like these can leave you paralyzed, stuck in a dark place. You can't even see your way out. These experiences and memories cause so much pain, and they can stagnate your life. It can keep you from living a victorious life in Jesus Christ. How do you get relief? How do you move forward?

If you are stuck on your journey in life because of a wrong that someone has done to you, you have to forgive in order to move forward. Forgiveness is a very important part of moving past pain.

It is the "key" in the ignition to jumpstart the process of getting on with your life. You can't carry bitterness in your heart and find healing and wholeness at the same time. You have to unload it, and give it to God. You can't move with a heavy load of bitterness. Bitterness makes it impossible to move freely. You may be able to move, but there will always be this burden on the inside of you, weighing you down, which in turn makes you move slowly. Bitterness is one of those things that has to be unpacked in your suitcase of life for you to move ahead with the journey that God has planned for you. Taking inventory of what is in that suitcase and seeing what is not needed will make your journey lighter and brighter.

Forgiving someone who has hurt you physically, emotionally, or both is very difficult to say the least. But with God's help, it's possible. Ask God to help you forgive by faith. That means asking God to help you forgive the offender and believing that He will give you strength to do it. Will you feel like it? No. Will you even want to forgive? Maybe not, but God tells us to in Matthew 6:14–15: "For if you forgive men their trespasses, your heavenly Father will also forgive you. But if you do not forgive men their trespasses, neither will your Father forgive your trespasses." We must forgive so that we can be forgiven.

Bitterness also hinders our prayers (Mark 11:25). And to be quite honest, nothing is worth hindering my communication with my Father. He is my life. Only in Him are we able to forgive. He will heal all wounds if we allow Him to. God is so awesome in how He works everything out for our good. Forgiving someone may be painful, but after the pain, you can finally have freedom! When you forgive, it's a heavy load lifted off of you. It's mainly for your benefit, not for the person who hurt you. What they did to hurt you is between them and God now. You are released and no longer in bondage. With God's help, you can do it! You will be able to release bitterness and all its buddies: resentment, anger, and hate.

Once you get rid of these bullies, you'll feel lighter, and you can move more freely. The dead weight is gone.

Another integral part of pushing forward is forgetting the past. There are some past memories that are happy, joyful, and even humorous. For some people it may be their wedding days, the births of babies, special memories with parents, graduations, or the first days of exciting jobs. These occasions and situations can bring back happy memories, and you enjoy reminiscing about these special events in your life. Then there are hurtful, painful, and upsetting experiences that you don't like to look back on. You try your best not to think back to those dreadful times, but the memories keep resurfacing. You might not think about the actual bad experiences, but they may manifest themselves in other ways such as relationships, addictions, and other behaviors. Being fearful and unable to trust, and feeling insecure, unworthy, anxious, and depressed are just some the ways that past hurts can affect your life now and later if you don't let go. Some people are not able to sustain good relationships due to intimacy or trust issues. Others may succumb to promiscuity because of sexual abuse. Others may turn to alcohol, drugs, or even food to dull the pain they have experienced in their pasts. All of these substitutes will never fill the void in their hearts. Only Jesus can fill it to overflow. Surrendering all to Jesus allows Him to flood your heart with His amazing love which heals all wounds.

Moving forward requires a total surrender of all that haunts, hurts, and angers you to God. Casting it all at His feet and leaving it there. Believing Him to help you to take continual steps forward to wholeness. He knows all about deep-rooted afflictions and He is able to heal to the utmost!

"Therefore, if anyone is in Christ, he is a new creation, old things have passed away; behold, all things have become new" (2 Cor.

5:17). We are new and restored when we are in Christ. All things are made new. Not, some things about us are made new, *all* things are made new. For example, I love going to resale shops. I enjoy looking around for deals on unique items. Sometimes I can find an item for a very good price, and the store is almost giving it away. It's a deal that I can't walk away from. Once I found two beautiful, cherry wood candle holders—my best find yet. All they needed was a little washing with a cloth, and they were like new.

Other times I may find something old but unique. It might be a little shabby and in need of work, like an old, worn chair. Some may have passed that chair by and thought it was useless. Somehow, I see value in that chair. This chair is worth something. The legs on the chair are wobbly. The arms of the chair have scrapes and scratches, and the upholstery is dull and torn in places. This chair looks like it has been through some things, but it has a unique beauty to it. If someone put some work into it, it could be restored elegantly. I'm no expert, but I think the wobbly legs could be fixed with a little glue, clamps, and nails. The scratches and scrapes on the arms of the chair can be sanded down, and a lustrous finish can be restored to the wood. The old upholstery can be removed and covered with a beautiful durable upholstery fabric. Restored like new! Beautiful, nice, and sturdy! A great find and almost free!

Before I came to Christ, I was torn, worn, wobbly, and had some scrapes and scratches, just like that old chair. God saw value in me and made me new. The price God paid for me is His Son. That is how much you and I are worth! You never lose value because the One who bought you, redeemed you with His precious blood.

When I accepted Christ as my Savior, He began to do a work in me, and the old things passed away. He didn't see me as useless like some saw that old chair. Like the chair covered with new fabric, God has arrayed me with the robe of righteousness and clothed me with the garments of salvation and they never wear out. (Isa. 61:10)! I was torn, and He mended my heart and healed my scratches, and

Prayer Matters

washed me with His blood! My legs were wobbly but now I stand firmly on the Word of God. He renewed my mind! I'm restored like new! I once told my testimony to a group of teenagers and someone came to me later on and said, "Not you, Sis. Shannon, you didn't do all those terrible things. Not you. I can't believe it." You see, when God restores you, you don't look the same to the people in your old life, and the new people in your life can't believe who you once were. The only time I reflect back on the bad in my life is when I'm helping someone to move forward with the good in their life. When you move forward, you are able to forget those things which are behind, reach forward to those things which are ahead, and press toward the goal for the prize of the upward call of God in Christ Jesus (Phil. 3:13–14)!

Prayer Matter

Father, God, I come to You in the precious name of Jesus. I thank You, Lord, that because of Jesus I can come before Your throne of grace and ask for help. Lord, I pray that You will help me to move forward from the hurts of my past. Enable me to forgive those who have done me harm. Lord, I really don't feel like forgiving them, but I know it's what You told me to do in your Word. I confess that I want them to hurt like I hurt. Lord, free from these feelings, and bring healing so that I may be free from them forever. I ask You to help me to forgive my offenders by faith. Father, I can't do it on my own. I release the person or persons who hurt me to You. They have no control over me or my life anymore. I release my hurts, pains, bitterness, and fears to You.

Lord, I want to trust again. I want to be free to love without having walls up. My desire is to have a normal, loving relationship. Lord, give me the desires of my heart according to Your will for my life. Father, I pray that you will bring good-hearted, kind, and spirit-filled people into my life. Enable me to not be deceived by people. Give me wisdom and discernment about people whom I allow into my life. Show me who they really are, Lord, and help me to discern their true intentions.

Father, where there are deep hurts and disappointments, I ask You to pour out Your comfort, peace, and joy. Bring healing to the secret, deep wounds that only You and I know about. Take away all discouragement, guilt, and sadness. Where my feet have been stuck in the mud of despair, I ask You to lift them out, and allow me to walk in the path that You have set before me. Restore to me hope, and encourage my heart.

Give me new eyes to look ahead and not behind me. I allow You to complete Your good work in me (Phil. 1:6). Father, instill in me a new zeal for life. Give me a new excitement and optimism for my future and life in You. I give You glory and honor. I carry on by faith! In Jesus's name, amen.

GOD'S CALL

Moreover whom He predestined, these he also called; whom He called, these He also justified; and whom He justified, these He also glorified.

—Romans 8:30

What am I here for? What was I created to do? Am I doing what I'm supposed to be doing with my life? Am I going in the right direction? Am I where I'm supposed to be? These questions have often danced around in my head during those times when I'm feeling like something is missing in my life, times when I'm not totally sure if I'm doing what God would have me to do. Sometimes I think that there has to be something more to life than this. I experience feelings of just not being satisfied.

These emotions of being unsure and in limbo are very common today. People often go out, seeking different things that they don't have the talent, interest, or gifting to do. I would try my hand at different things, attempt various jobs, take various classes, or approach a different church, not really knowing what I wanted to do. More importantly, I had no idea what God wanted me to do. I had no direction or vision, and the Bible says in Proverbs 29:18, "Where there is no vision, people perish." This verse describes exactly I how felt: like I was just living my life day to day. I was moving in many directions but going nowhere.

All the time, I was lost on the inside because I had no direction. I felt in my spirit that there was something in me that was great and unique that God wanted me to do for Him. There was a tugging in my spirit; He was calling me to something, and He is calling you, too. Will you ignore the call or answer it? Maybe you put Him on hold because you are not ready. Or maybe you are just not sure you are answering the right call, and you start to doubt. Or it could be that you have so many voices telling you to go this way or that way, and you don't know which way to go because you're so confused. Maybe you feel like God can't use you or that you are not good enough. However, you were created for a specific, unique purpose, and God has a plan for you.

If we are in Christ, we each have a holy calling from God: "Who has saved us and called us with a holy calling, not according to our works, but according to His own purpose and grace which was given to us in Christ Jesus before time" (2 Tim. 1:9). God offers us the free gift of salvation. God draws us to Him. In John 6:44, Jesus says, "No one can come to Me unless the Father who sent Me draws him; and I will raise him up at the last day." God first draws us into salvation by His Spirit. God pulls at our hearts, teaches us, and shows us His faithfulness and goodness: "But you are a chosen generation, a royal priesthood, a holy nation, His own special people, that you may proclaim the praise of Him who called you out of darkness into His marvelous light" (1 Pet. 2:9). When we understand and yearn for relationships with Him, we accept Christ as our Savior and invite Him into our hearts. We lay down our lives so that we can live totally for Him. In the process of living for

Prayer Matters

God, we are being sanctified. We are each in the process of taking off the old man, putting on the new man, being renewed in our minds (Eph. 4:22–24). In this scripture the Apostle Paul compares our Christian life to clothes. Taking off the dirty clothes of our sinful past and putting on new clothes made of Christ's righteousness. We can't do it on our own, we need the Holy Spirit. The Holy Spirit helps us, and we begin to walk in the Spirit and not seek after our own fleshly desires. As we walk in the Spirit, our hearts are cleansed, and we are washed continually, preparing for His purpose. Do we mess up and make mistakes? Yes, but thank God for grace, another day, another chance. God does expect us to live a consistent, Christian lifestyle, but He also knows our frame and remembers that we are just dust (Ps. 103:14).

It's God's grace that helps us to do what we can't do on our own. Our callings are not based on how noble or good we are; they're based on how great and worthy God is. We may feel inappropriate and inadequate, but we are made suitable by the Holy Spirit. It is the work of the Holy Spirit that equips Jesus for ministry. Acts 10:38 says, "How God anointed Jesus of Nazareth with the Holy Spirit and with power, who went about doing good and healing all who were oppressed by the devil, for God was with Him." You may say, "That was Jesus." I'm here to tell you that the same anointing of the Holy Spirit that equipped Jesus for service is the same anointing that equips you for ministry. 2 Corinthians 1:21–22 says, "Now He who establishes us with you in Christ and has anointed us is God, who also has sealed us and given us the Spirit in our hearts as a guarantee." If we are in Christ, God gives us special endowment of the Holy Spirit to fulfill His call in our lives. God just needs us to be willing.

You have to love people in order to be an effective servant to God and others. To really love people is to serve others with love. We must share the gospel message of Jesus Christ so that people can be saved. And may I add that this is an emergency situation? Time is short, so choosing to stay in our comfort zones should never be an option. Most times, I would rather stay in my comfort zone, around the people I know and care about. For the most part, I'm not an outgoing person, I guess you could call me an introvert. But God has placed me in situations where I have had to initiate prayer, give my testimony, lead groups, conduct home bible study and outreaches. I'm having to get out of my comfort zone and into the zone that God wants me in. The more I do it, the more comfortable I am, and the bonus is that I'm always blessed by it. God will impart love and an interest in others to you as you seek His heart. The love He pours into you will overflow onto others through you. You will have compassion for others instead of judgment. You won't look down on others; instead, you will be compelled to help. You won't give up on people because their lives depend on it. God has placed His love and gifts in you to touch the hearts of others for Him. It's all birthed out of the love and compassion He places in your heart. Again, you have to be willing. Is it comfortable at first? No, but God is getting you to where He wants you to be, and surrendering to Him in obedience every step of the way will get you there. Depend on Him for all you need.

God's transforming power is real. When I first became a believer, my prayers were mostly focused on myself. My prayers were for me and my family and my friends. As I grew and matured in Christ, my life changed. As I sought God, my heart for people began to change. You know how people say, "When you've been around someone so long, you start to look and act like them." Well, if you are in a true, sincere relationship with God, you will start to take on His attributes and qualities. You start to take on His love and concern for others. Thinking only of yourself and the people who are close to you will be a thing of the past. Praying only for your inner circle is over and done with. Your inner circle expands to your church, neighborhoods, government, missionaries, and the world.

Prayer Matters

Being a Christian and not living out your God-ordained purpose is like baking a cake and leaving out an essential ingredient. You have all the ingredients for a tasty cake. Let's see, people have said that I make a good pound cake, so I'll use that for an illustration. I gather the butter, sugar, cake flour, vanilla extract, and eggs. I mix everything perfectly, gently adding one egg at time. After a few minutes of mixing, I taste it and it tastes pretty good. I spray my pan and carefully pour the batter into my cake pan, place it in the oven, and let it bake. The aroma fills the house, and the fragrance is causing much anticipation from my husband and kids. After a while in the oven, Mama's famous pound cake is ready. I take it out of the oven, and I look at it. It looks flat, like it has no substance. Ummm...what is missing? Something is missing. What would keep the cake from rising? I forgot to add the baking powder. Will it still taste good? Yes. Will my family still eat it? Absolutely. They won't know that something on the inside of the cake is missing. Its taste is good, but it just didn't rise. That's the way it is with our calling, but on a spiritual level. As believers, we can be going through the motions of going to church, reading our Bibles, and going to family nights, small groups, etc., but still something is missing, and we can't rise up in our purposes until we discover what it is we were made for. And until you determine what it is, you'll exist, but you won't be whole—no substance, flat. Only through the Spirit of God will it be revealed to you, and you will come alive inside, and rise to all that God has called you to be.

This is how I knew my calling. I had a strong desire to pray for others. This led me to study the Bible more and read books about intercession. I began to learn how to pray more effectively. I so wanted to pray the effectual fervent prayer of the righteous that avail much (James 5:16). It was only the love of God that flooded my heart to cry out before Him for others. Only God could have taken my eyes off myself and placed people in my heart who needed Him. My hunger and thirst to pray on the behalf of others grew. It was placed inside me by God, and I had to do it. I had a pulling on my heart, a strong desire to pray for others. I wanted to encourage them and bring them comfort through the word of God. All believers are called to go out and fulfill the Great Commission, but even more was my desire to intercede. I sought God, and I continue to ask Him to teach me how to serve Him and to teach me how to pray.

Eventually, God started to place people in my heart out of nowhere. I mean, I wouldn't even be thinking about the person, and the Holy Spirit would lead me to call and pray for them. I am not a phone person at all, so this took a lot of effort and courage to call somebody out of the blue and ask them if I could pray for them. Sometimes I would resist, but the Holy Spirit would not leave me alone. It's like I had to do it, or I wouldn't have any peace. So, eventually, I would give in, but it was a fight that I was going to lose anyway. I would hesitantly and nervously call the person whom God placed on my heart to call and pray with. I'm so thankful to God that I was obedient. Most times the person on the other end needed prayer at that very moment. I would even call people who were sick or going in for surgery. I had no idea, and they assumed I knew, but I didn't. God did! I'm always encouraged when this happens because I know that I am hearing from the Holy Spirit. See, there is no need to be afraid or feel like you are not good enough. God will give you His grace and strength, and He will put His words in your mouth. He will never call you to do something that you can't do. He will equip you for everything needed to do His work (Heb. 13:21). Don't labor so much in your own strength. Believe me, you will wear yourself out trying to do the work. It's God job to work through you, and you must depend totally on Him to do it. Ask the Holy Spirit to be released through you, and trust Him to work through you to complete the work that God purposed for you to do from the beginning of time.

God calls on the prophet Jeremiah. He says, "Before I formed you in the womb I knew you; Before you were born I sanctified you; I ordained you to be a prophet to the nations." Jeremiah's call to ministry was to be a prophet. Before he was born, God had determined that he would be a prophet. I ponder that in my mind: "before he was born." Before you were even born, God predestined you for a special calling and gifting. That is so awesome! My mind can't conceive of it. God is so marvelous, wonderful, and big, that there is no word to describe His awesomeness! God already had plans for you before you were even born. The plans He has for you are preordained (Rom. 8:29). God is strategic, and you are an important part of His plan. In order to discover what piece you are in His plan, you have to seek Him. Seeking Him involves getting in His Word, spending time in His presence, praying, and yielding and surrendering to His will. As you consistently walk in the Spirit, God will start to move you in the right direction. As you move in that direction, the more eager you will be to do it. You will develop a passion for it. However, if you are moving in the wrong direction, you may feel unsettled and not have peace about it.

For example, when I was a new believer, I really wanted to get involved in a ministry. I was excited about serving the Lord in some capacity. I wound up getting involved a number of ministries. If someone asked me to join, most times I would join. One ministry in particular was the "Building and Improvement Committee." It was a great ministry, but I had no interest in architecture, painting, repairing, or reconstruction of the church. Now, my husband is very good at all of those things, and they come quite naturally for him. But me? No way! I did join the choir, and I loved singing and praising the Lord in song. When you start to press into your calling, you'll know it in your heart. The Spirit of God will settle it in your heart, and you'll have peace about it. You will feel whole, fulfilled, and complete. Will there be some bumps in the road? Yes. But you'll know without a shadow of a doubt that you are doing what you were born to do for His kingdom and for His glory. You will be enthusiastic, optimistic, and excited! Partner with the Holy Spirit and He will lead you into a future that is full of overabundant grace that will help you to serve and advance His kingdom.

Prayer Matter

Father, I thank You for creating me. Not only did You create me, but you had a reason behind it. You created me for a specific purpose, something that only I can do especially for You. Holy Spirit, I ask that you would pour out Your Spirit upon me. May Your Living Water rain on all of my dry places and awaken me to know what I was created for. Let there be a refreshing in my spirit, Lord.

Father, reveal to me any unknown strengths, interests, and gifts I may have. Open up doors of opportunity that will lead me in the direction of my purpose. When the doors are open, give me boldness and strength to walk through them. Father, take away all fear. I know you have not given me a spirit of fear, Lord, but of power, love, and a sound mind (2 Tim. 1:7). I release my feelings of insecurity and doubt to You. Replace these feelings with holy boldness, enthusiasm, optimism, and a strong desire to spread the good news of the gospel of Jesus Christ. I receive Your grace to enable me to do all that you created me to do with excellence and humility. May I always be pressing on to the upward call of You in Christ Jesus (Phil. 3:14).

Give me Your love for people. I know that love is the motivating factor, for You are love. Open my spiritual eyes and ears to see and hear You more clearly. Enlighten my eyes with understanding so that I may know the hope of your calling for my life (Eph. 1:18). Give me a hunger and thirst for Your word, and I pray that it will come alive to me and give me direction.

Father, I thank You that I have been called with a holy calling. I answer "Lord, yes." I surrender my will for Your will. I yield and surrender all at Your feet. I am Yours, Lord, and I know You are mine. May all that You pour into me be poured out to others by Your Spirit through me. May every gift and talent that You placed in me be awakened by Your Spirit, for Your glory. In Jesus's name, amen.

SELF-CONTROL

No chastening seems to be joyful for the present, but pain-
ful; nevertheless, afterward it yields the peaceable fruit of
righteousness to those who have been trained by it.

—Hebrews 12:11

D o you have something or somethings in your life that you just can't seem to have discipline about? If you have just a little or do it just a little bit, do you completely go over the edge? It's like once you start, that red light does not come on? If you do, then you are not alone. We all have some weaknesses in our lives that we just can't seem to gain control over. For some it might be romantic partners, like that man you've been dating. You know in your heart that he is not God's best for you, but you settle because the attraction is so strong. You think that your biological clock has ticked out. Or you may feel like that old song, "I'm So Tired of Being Alone."

While some may be settling for "Mr. Right Now," others may like to shop. They go in the store and no matter how hard they try not to buy those red pumps, they buy them, even though they have three similar pairs at home. They impulse buy on the clearance rack and buy in bulk the things that they don't need.

Some people can't control their anger. When they are bothered by people or difficult situations, they blow up. Controlling their mouths is an issue for some, who say whatever is on their minds.

Disciplining oneself to exercise is a challenge for a lot of people. A big one for me and a lot of other Americans is food. Some have even taken on the title of "foodie." In other words, you love to eat. Unfortunately, a lot of people are obese. Addictions to food, alcohol, drugs, social media, caffeine, gambling, hoarding, and even the approval of others are all common areas that people have issues with. If you can't control the things that you have no power over, they will overpower you, and you could end up in a lot of trouble down the line. When we are out of control, we need to develop self-control. Jesus left us the Helper, the Holy Spirit, to help us when we can't help ourselves. Cooperating and co-partnering with the Holy Spirit will help us to gain victory over those vices that have us out of control.

Everything Jesus did on earth was by the power of the Holy Spirit, God's power. Acts 10:38 says, "How God anointed Jesus of Nazareth with the Holy Spirit and with power, who went about doing good and healing all who were oppressed by the devil, for God was with Him." Jesus goes about healing, teaching, preaching, and spreading the gospel all in the power of the Holy Spirit. That same power is available for us today to help us to be empowered by His Spirit.

One of the works of the Holy Spirit is to help us. He is our Helper (John 14:26). Jesus says in John 14:16–18,

And I will pray the Father, and He will give you another Helper, that He may abide with you forever, the Spirit of truth, whom the world cannot receive, because it neither sees Him nor knows Him; but you know Him for He dwells with you and will be in you. I will not leave you orphans; I will come to you.

The Spirit of truth is the Holy Spirit. If you are in Christ, the Holy Spirit lives in you. It is the power of God living in you to help you to do the things that you can't do on your own.

The scripture says in Philippians 2:13, "for it is God who works in you both to will and to do for His good pleasure." It is God who works in us to bring about change in us for His pleasure. Only by the power of the Spirit can we live disciplined lives that bring about transformations that last. Trying in our own strengths leads to frustration, discouragement, and no change that lasts. You experience victory in an area awhile, and then you find yourself getting weak because you are doing it in your own power. Gradually, you end up right back where you started.

I've been in this place so many times. In these times, you feel like you are a failure, and even worse, you feel like you've failed God. The feelings of hopelessness, guilt, and shame are quite overwhelming—quite unlike the feelings I felt while I was taking part in things that I was trying not to do. While I was doing something forbidden, it was fun, exciting, and seemed fulfilling. But afterward, I felt horrible, and condemnation would eat me up inside. Each time I felt like it wasn't worth it, only to go back and do it again.

In my life, I've struggled with many vices that I had no control over, from alcohol to cigarettes to food. I've even had some issues with my mouth, saying things that were not edifying. My battles to stop drinking and overeating have been the most difficult. Quitting smoking was hard at first, but as I mentioned earlier God took the taste away. I hate—I mean *strongly* hate—the smell of cigarettes now. I literally will get sick to my stomach, and in some strange way I appreciate that because I know that's something I will never go back to. It makes me ill to even think about it. Now, the alcohol was another complete story.

My battle with alcohol as you know was long and hard. After many times of stopping and going back to it, eventually I had a strong desire to quit. God was dealing with me about it. He would not let me be comfortable doing it. You know that strong conviction, nudging you to get yourself together? I seriously determined in my mind that I was going to quit. At first, I would have weeks of sobriety. I reflect back now and remember how I thought one week or two weeks was a long time for me, a huge victory. I eventually went months, then the months turned into a year, and then a year turned into two years. Unfortunately, after two years of being sober, I went back to drinking. Was it every day? No, just on special occasions like holidays, or family functions. I didn't think it was that bad. I didn't do it all the time. Just these "special" days wouldn't bother me. The devil is and always will be a liar. I was trying to convince myself that it was OK for me. Don't get me wrong. I'm not the "no drinking" police. We as believers are not to get drunk (Eph. 5:18). But for me, it was not good for me to drink any alcoholic beverage. Most times I did not recognize the "red light" telling me to stop or that I'd had enough. In the rare times that I did stop, I still desired more. I even convinced myself that wine would be OK. I got off the strong alcohol and said, "I'll only drink wine. It's in the Bible, right?" This is how I would try to minimize my addiction. Well, I started to drink wine...and more wine...and more wine. I was trying to get that feeling, and in order to get that feeling and get it quick, I went back to the hard stuff. It only takes a little of the hard to stuff to get you "there" quick, I rationalized in my head. I asked myself, "How did I get here again?" After two years, I couldn't believe I went back into the horrible pit that had the disgusting stench of gloom, depression, booze, and hopelessness.

Prayer Matters

I still remember the repulsive taste that I struggled to get out of my mouth after a binge: dry, repulsive, and evil. I hated it, but I would soon be back at it. Trying to get that feeling; again.

I cried out to God and told Him, "Lord I'm tired of this; I'm tired of struggling in my own strength. I'm tired of being sick and hungover. I'm tired of going through this cycle over and over. I'm tired of the pain. Take it away from me." I was so ashamed and guilty before God, and I thought He looked at me with shame. Let me tell you, I know now that He was not looking at me that way at all. He loved me and never stopped loving me. God is a merciful God, and He wants His best for all of us. Sure, He was not pleased with me, but He loved me and was there to help me. I just had to be willing.

I needed to take the way of escape and that way is in Him (1 Cor. 10:13). In the past, I took the way I wanted to go. When I was stressed, I took my own way. When I was upset about something, I took my own way. When I just wanted to have a good time, I took my own way. But God kept dealing with me. Not until I got tired—I mean really tired—of the cycle did I make the decision that I was going to stop drinking for real. I needed God's help to do it. I tried my way, now it was time to try God's way. I was totally depending on Him and His sufficient grace to help once and for all.

The Bible says in Ephesians 6:12, "For we do not wrestle against flesh and blood, but against principalities, against powers, against the rulers of the darkness of this age, against spiritual wickedness in heavenly places." This battle that I had with addiction was a spiritual battle. Alcohol was a stronghold for me; I mean it had a *strong* hold on me, and I couldn't break free on my own. It took a sincere, desperate surrender, making a serious decision that I wanted to stop drinking, and asking God for His help to do it. It took a made-up mind. Since we don't fight against flesh and blood, how do we fight? We fight in the spirit realm through prayer, and we are to take up the whole armor of God (Eph. 6:13-18). There are six pieces of spiritual armor.

The first piece of armor girds your waist with truth. I had to be honest and truthful with myself and especially with God. It's hard taking a good look at yourself and not liking what you see, but the truth of the matter is, examining yourself and admitting that you have a problem is needed for the fight. I had no control over alcohol, and I needed God's help to get victory over it. I had to be honest with myself and admit that I had a problem. No rationalizing or compromising, and no thinking, "I only drink on weekends, so I don't have a problem." This was a lie from Satan, and I fell for it. To be honest, I just wanted to "feel good" at the time. Yes, most times I only drank on weekends, but believe me, what I didn't drink during week, I made up for on the weekend. Another lie from the enemy was, "If I only drink wine instead of the 'hard stuff,' it's OK." No, it was not OK for me. I'd drink a glass of wine and it would turn into a bottle or two. I had to reject the lies and receive the truth in God's word in order to break free from the deception and the power alcohol had over me. Jesus is the Way, the Truth and the Light (John 14:6). Jesus came to set the captives free, and I needed to be set free; for real. The only way I was going to get true freedom was through Him (Luke 4:18).

Fully submitting to God and being truthful to myself and others was needed in order for me to gain victory over alcohol. It was important for me to be truthful with my husband and my kids. I tried for so long to hide drinking from them. I would only drink a little in their presence, but I always had me a bottle hidden somewhere. At least, I thought it was hidden. My oldest daughter would find it and pour out most of my alcohol, then replace the rest with water. She would also tear up my cigarettes. It's funny, after my youngest daughter found out about my "sneak drinks" she told me, "Ma, I had no idea you used to drink that much." I guess I tried

Prayer Matters

to hide it well, but I couldn't hide from myself, and I definitely couldn't hide from God.

The second piece of armor is the breastplate of righteousness (Eph. 6:14). The breastplate protects our hearts from the assaults of Satan, from the lies he tells. This righteousness is not of our own but the righteousness of Christ. We have been made righteous through the shed blood of Jesus Christ (2 Cor. 5:21). So as long as we put on our breastplates of righteousness, our hearts are protected against the attacks of the enemy because we know we were made righteous by our Savior.

The third piece of armor is having our feet shod with the preparation of the gospel of peace (Eph. 6:15). We must put on these spiritual shoes so that we can stand firm and steady in battle. As we walk by faith with God, there are going to be enemy traps to discourage us and to keep us from spreading the gospel. We can't give Satan any ground. I gave Satan ground by continuing to give in to temptation. I could not be an effective witness for spreading the gospel if I was bound myself. In order to help others to be free, you must be free. Once free, you will have peace with God through Jesus Christ. It's so important to have our feet ready and prepared so that we may be able to stand firmly on the path that God has for us.

The fourth piece is found in Ephesians 6:16: "Above all, taking the shield of faith with which you will be able to quench all the fiery darts of the wicked one." This piece of armor is very significant because the scripture starts with "above all," implying utter importance. When we place our faith in God and in His word, Satan's fiery darts are extinguished. When I was tempted to drink, I had to have faith in God and His promises. I had to believe that I could do all things through Christ who strengthens me (Phil. 4:13). I had to have faith that God's grace was and is sufficient for me, and that His strength is made perfect in my weakness (2 Cor.

12:9). When you have unwavering faith and trust in God, you are protected against the enemy, and his fiery darts cannot touch you.

We must take the helmet of salvation and the sword of the Spirit (Eph. 6:17). The helmet of salvation protects the mind. It's crucial that we put on the helmet of salvation. Satan will try to gain control of your mind and thoughts. He'll have you thinking to yourself, "I'm a failure and I'll never be able to break this vicious cycle. I might as well give up. I'm never going to be able to break free. God doesn't love me. Look at me, I'm a mess." Oh, the guilt, shame condemnation, and depression would torment me. The enemy was tormenting me and I had no peace. In fact, I was in turmoil. I needed my helmet on and I mean, I needed my helmet on *bad.* I thought that God didn't love me and that He gave up on me. Lies! The enemy will try to blind you from the truth. That's why you must know the word of God, the sword of the Spirit. It's very important to believe the word of God He has for us in the Bible. Although I was bound, God still loved me, and there was nothing that I could do that would stop Him from loving, caring, and wanting His best for me: "But God, who is rich in mercy, because of His great love with which He loved us, even when we were dead in trespasses, made us alive together with Christ (by grace you have been saved)" (Eph. 2:4–5). I'm so thankful to God for His love and for His abounding mercy. In my sin, He loved me, and He loved me so much that He brought me out of that sin, and I can't give Him enough thanks and praise for that.

Prayer is last piece of armor mentioned in this passage: "Praying always with all prayer and supplication in the Spirit" (Eph. 6:18). Praying the mind of God and from the word of God empowers us for victory. The Holy Spirit helps us to pray when we may not know what to pray. He prays for us with groanings that cannot be expressed. (Rom. 8:26) Pray for God's will to be done. It was not His will for me to be in bondage; it was His will for me to walk in the liberty that Jesus gave His life for me to have (John 8:36). Prayer

Prayer Matters

gives you strength to endure when trials or temptations come, and most importantly, prayer invites God into the situation and allows for Him to move on your behalf.

Jesus is the permanent fix for temporary situations. Jesus could do nothing without with the Father and neither can we (John 5:19). It takes coming to the end of yourself and what your flesh wants to finally have a sincere desire to please God. Our love for God will compel us to walk out our victory. Nothing is worth not living out His plans and purposes for our lives. Furthermore, you won't have any peace until you lay whatever it is down that is hindering you from being who God created you to be. Now that I am sober, I have the peaceable fruit of righteousness, and nothing can compare to that.

Setting goals is very helpful in cultivating self-control. Goals help you to visualize where you want to be. Having strategic steps in place will enable you to reach your desired destinations. This takes work on your part. You do your part, and God does His part. It will take continuously trusting and believing in God, and with God all things are possible (Matt. 19:26). The key word that I would like to focus on is "with." All things are possible with God, meaning that it cannot happen without Him. Only He can bring about change in us that will last so that He may be glorified through us.

Whether we need to stop partaking in something completely, stop doing things in excess, let go of unhealthy relationships, or discipline ourselves in certain areas, we need the Lord. Seek the Lord in prayer for strength and guidance. If we are powerless to alcohol, we need to stop indulging in it. But what about food? We need food to live. Asking God to help you make healthier food choices and praying against the spirit of gluttony will help in this area. Have I gained total victory in this area? As of my writing this very moment, not total victory, but I am well on my way. With God's help, I know I can do it. It's always good to look at the benefits of achieving self-control in problematic areas. I know that for me, when I exercise, I feel better, and I have more energy. I have more mind clarity. An extra perk is that I look better: My skin is clearer, I'm more toned, and I feel better about myself. A benefit of self-control with shopping is that you have extra money to save, or the money can be used in a more beneficial way like donating to a women's shelter. Maybe you can even start cleaning out that closet of clothes that you never wear. Give away some clothes or shoes that you don't wear to women in need. Believe me, letting go of things is hard. I have those clothes in the back of my closet that I never wear and probably will never wear, but someone could use them. Why not bless someone with them?

Maybe some of the time spent on social media could be used by actually socializing with people in person, perhaps by visiting the sick or volunteering. There have been times when I have spent too much time on social media, scrolling and snooping. I've watched so many YouTube tutorials, I should be a makeup expert, but I had to start making better use of my time. I determined that I was wasting a lot of time, and that time could be well spent by studying and reading my Bible more. I could also call someone to encourage and pray with them. Yes, we are to have recreation time, and I love recreation, but we do have to realize that too much of something can be a major distraction in our lives. Making better use of time and finding opportunities to be a blessing to someone will cause a shift in our priorities and perspectives, and it also takes the focus off of ourselves and our issues. It helps us to lead more balanced, productive lives for the glory of God.

Matthew 7:22 says, "Ask, and it will be given to you; seek, and you will find; knock, and it will be opened to you. For everyone who asks receives, and he who seeks finds, and to him who knocks it will be opened." First, you have to resolve in your mind that you are really ready for change. You must be willing and ready to take the steps to achieve the desired result. Secondly, you have to ask and believe that God will give you what you ask for. Then, you have to seek Him. Seek Him in prayer, and ask the Holy Spirit to clothe

Prayer Matters

you with power to withstand the temptation. Cry out to Him in desperation, giving it all to Him. He already knows your heart. He knows that you have been trying and failing. He knows that you want to please Him, but your flesh is weak. He knows that you're tired and His arms are wide open to receive you and give you rest and deliverance. This is where you find Him. He's been there all along, He's just been waiting to receive you and give you the power from on high to put your life together the way He purposed for it to be: to be fully controlled by His Spirit, not by our flesh, by the world, nor by the schemes of the enemy.

Being renewed in our minds brings about transformation. When we are devoted to God's truths and allow the Holy Spirit to guide and construct our thoughts, it prompts a change in our hearts, and then our actions will change. The more we rely on the Holy Spirit, the more we are able to walk with God in power and be saved from self and self's desires: "For you died, and your life is hidden with Christ in God" (Col. 3:3). Our lives must be committed to what God wants, relinquishing what we can't control to God. There is no self-control without the power from above to control ourselves. We are the vehicle; the vehicle can't move without the gas to give it power. The Holy Spirit poured into us is the "gas" that gets us moving in the right direction. We steer the steering wheel, but He tells us which way to turn and guides us in the right direction. We are totally dependent on the Holy Spirit to control this vehicle. Without Him, we are going nowhere.

As we seek Him, our desire to please Him will grow stronger. Being out of control will deplete us spiritually, emotionally, and physically. In order to gain self-control, we have to give God total control. As we give Him control and seek Him, the life that God has planned for us that was once hidden will start to be revealed. We will start to walk and live out our purpose. You will realize that the thing that you had no control over was just a substitute for the real thing. It was a void that you were trying to fill with something

115

or someone that was not meant to be used as a filler. No matter how much you filled it with the substitute, it was never enough. It was a foreign substance, and it left you out of control with no fulfillment. What was needed was a true filling of the Holy Spirit, a continual flow of Living Water that empowers you, satisfying your deepest inner thirst. Only then will you function at your best and your life will be like a tree planted by the stream of water which brings forth fruit in due season! (Jer. 17:8)

Prayer Matter

Father, I thank You for your treasured gift of self-control. I direct my heart to You, Lord, and ask that You reveal to me any areas in my life that are out of control. I ask you to help me to gain freedom over areas of my life where I have no restraint. I'm so tired of battling to stop doing things that are not pleasing to You. I've tried so many times in my own strength—so many times, I can't even count them. I release all things in my life that I have no control over to You. Father, what I will to do, I don't do (Rom. 7:15.) I need You to help me to gain lasting victory in my life.

I confess that I have made things or people idols in my life. I've chosen to go my own way, walking after my own earthly desires. Forgive me, Lord, when I've placed things or people before You. Deliver me from my own selfish desires. May my foremost hunger and desire be for You. When tempted, may I be mindful to take the way of escape (1 Cor. 10:13). Give me strength to lay down anything that has me bound at Your altar, and as I lay it down may I be determined and faithful not to pick it up again.

Only You can make changes in me that last. I surrender all to You. I take up the shield of faith so that I will be able to quench all the fiery darts of the wicked one. Through faith in God Almighty, I am shielded from the enemy's fiery darts. I put on the helmet of salvation to protect my mind from the lies, deceptions, and temptations of the enemy. I put on the breastplate of righteousness; I am the righteousness of God. I gird my waist with truth. Your Word is true, and may it be unto me according to Your Word. I shod my feet with the preparation of the gospel. I stand firm, strong, and ready

Prayer Matters

for battle. I will live out the gospel and spread the gospel message to others through the peace that Jesus Christ has given me. I take up the Sword of the Spirit, the Word of God. I believe the Word, receive the Word, speak the Word, and pray the Word. I pray always with prayer and supplication in the Spirit with perseverance and I pray for all of the saints. I thank You, Lord, for providing everything that I need to stand. No weapon formed against me shall prosper because I am covered with the whole armor of God (Isa. 54:17). Thank You, Lord. In Jesus's name I pray, amen.

GOD'S UNFAILING LOVE

For God so loved the world that He gave His only begotten
Son, that whoever believes in Him should not perish but
have everlasting life.

—John 3:16

John 3:16 is one of, if not *the,* most known and quoted scripture. It's often quoted in speeches on Easter by children giving their speeches and is often a scripture that had to be memorized in Sunday school. Many sermons have been preached from this scripture. Although I'm very familiar with this scripture, I never really had a true revelation about the love of God until about five years ago. I was sitting in church, waiting for the service to begin, when the pastor's wife walked by me and said, "God loves you." She said it in such a way that it felt like God was speaking directly to me through her. He reassured me that He loved me, and at that moment I received His

Prayer Matters

love so effortlessly. It was so natural, like breathing in fresh morning air, at that moment I knew for a fact that He loved me. It was like my life changed all of a sudden. How could something so simple take so long to understand and receive? In my mind and heart, I was feeling like, "God loves *me*?" I was a person so broken. My life wasn't right; I was bound, but I knew in that very moment that God loved me anyway. No matter how dirty, shameful, and messed up I felt I was, He loved me and I felt it. It was like He poured a heavenly portion of His majestic love in my heart. It was so warm, comforting and assuring. I have never felt a more glorious love; God's love. There are no words grand enough to describe it.

At the time I had this revelation of God's love I was still in habitual sin, trying my best to get out of it, but God said, "I love you; it is finished." God didn't see what I saw when He looked at me. He saw His child who was created in His image, and although I wasn't right, He considered me worthy of giving His only begotten Son for me. He loves us all with a love that we can't even comprehend (Eph. 3:19). The magnitude of God's eternal love can't be measured. No words in any language can describe how deep and how definite His love is for us. His love is from everlasting to everlasting, and it does not fail. Human love fails, disappoints, and changes. God's love never runs out; there is an uninterrupted, endless flow of His majestic love that overflows to depths beyond comprehension (Ps. 136:1). His love for His children cannot be exhausted. If there is one thing you should know for sure with absolute certainty, is that God loves you—yes, you!

My strongest sense of love that I'd experienced up until this time in my life is when I had my first child. I went through twelve hours of excruciating labor. When I finally delivered her, I looked at her. She was covered with afterbirth, her skin wrinkly, eyes tightened, and head shaped a little funny. Even though she looked awkward, she was the most beautiful thing I had ever seen. I couldn't tell if she looked more like me or like my husband yet. All I knew was that I had never felt a love like that before. She was mine, a part of me, a miracle. When the nurses cleaned her up and handed her to me, I looked at her and felt a strong sense of affection, adoration, and an indescribable love that was immediate, automatic, and so natural. These feelings were new to me. My desire was to love, nurture, teach, provide, and protect her. With my second child, my feelings were exactly the same all over again. I love my children with a never-ending love. Do they do things that I don't like or agree with? Yes. Have they ever disappointed me? Yes, but nothing can stop me from loving them. As a mother, I want the best for them. When they hurt, I hurt. Even when they were younger and my husband and I would discipline them, it hurt me, but it was for their own good. They would thank us later on in their lives for the discipline because it kept them from making wrong decisions later on. God deals with us in the same way. "My son, do not despise the chastening of the Lord, Nor be discouraged when you are rebuked by Him; For whom the Lord loves He chastens, and scourges every son whom He receives." Sounds familiar—I can remember my mom saying, "I'm only whooping you because I love you." If you really love, you will correct. Correction now beats corruption later.

God knew us before we were in our mothers' wombs. Romans 8:29 says, "For whom He foreknew, He also predestined to be conformed to the image of His Son, that we might be the firstborn among many brethren." God knew beforehand that He wanted you to be His child and that you would be conformed to the image of His Son. His plans for you did not change just because you continued in sin, and neither did His love, just as my love for my child did not waver when she was born—even though she looked a little weird, her head shaped like a cone, covered in afterbirth. I loved her just the same as when the nurse cleaned her up. God loves the BC (before Christ) you and AC (after Christ) you just the same. He is that merciful. Not until we are born again in the Spirit and become His children does He start to clean us up. Our lives start to look different, and spiritual transformation starts to take place. Then we start to take on His attributes. I couldn't tell who my daughter looked like until she was cleaned up. Then I saw that she looked like my husband. As the days went by, her appearance started to change. It is a process of cleaning, washing, taking off the old, putting on the new; sanctification. As we grow and mature in Christ, our features and characteristics start to change. We start to look more like our Heavenly Father. Through this whole process, His love stays the same.

Do we mess up? Yes. We repent, ask for forgiveness, and keep it moving, knowing that God still loves us. "Who shall separate us from the love of Christ? Shall tribulation, distress, or persecution, or famine, or nakedness, or peril, or sword?" (Rom. 9:35).

> Yet in all these things we are more than conquerors through Him who loved us. For I am persuaded that neither death nor life, nor angels, nor principalities nor powers, nor things present nor things to come, nor height nor depth, nor any other created thing, shall separate us from the love of God which is in Christ Jesus our Lord. (Rom. 9:37–39)

That covers everything; absolutely nothing can separate us from the love of God.

I've come across so many young people who have been abandoned by a parent or by both parents. They feel rejected and unloved by the main people who should've been there for them to provide, love, nurture, and protect them. They have no idea what it feels like to be loved. So many end up seeking love in the world, only to be disappointed and hurt even more, causing their wounds to go deeper and deeper. In order to feel accepted and loved, they give in to peer pressure, gangs, alcohol, drugs, and promiscuity. Desperately seeking love that they never had, sometimes they wind up being used and mistreated. Deception and the need to be wanted leads them to believe that any attention, even negative attention, is better than no attention at all. How can they know what true love is if they've never gotten it? They don't know what it is so they are not able to give it, and they have a difficult time receiving it when someone comes along and genuinely loves and cares about them.

When we see the disrespectful child, the mean child, or the bully, there is usually a hurt, wounded child inside. These children have shut the doors of their hearts, and they find it hard to trust people. If people come along wanting to give them genuine love and care, it's difficult for them to allow them in. See, these doors they have under lock and key; they won't open. They're protective security doors that prevent them from being hurt. If you don't let people in, you can't get hurt. If only they knew that they have an Everlasting Father in heaven who loves and cares for them so much. It's crucial that we give out to others what God gives to us. Love will draw others in more than anything. When others see the love of Christ in us, they will be drawn to Him. Wounds are healed when love is the salve. Even when it's hard to show love to the unlovely, God living in us will give us the mercy, compassion, and grace to do so. God has great love for us, and we should have great love for others (Jer. 31:3). If God lives in us, we are able to love, for God is love: "He who does not love does not know God, for God is love" (1 John 4:8).

His love never fails, and His love is not based on our worthiness but is based on who God is. It is in His nature to love; He is love. Paul's description of love in 1 Corinthians 13:4–7 brings to life what true love really is. He says,

Love suffers long and is kind; love does not envy; love does not parade itself, it is not puffed up; does not behave rudely, does not seek his own, is not provoked, thinks no evil; does not rejoice in iniquity, but rejoices in the truth, bears all things, believes all things, hopes all things, endures all things.

Prayer Matters

The love described in this scripture is a love that does not think of self. It overwhelms me when I really think about all that love encompasses. Love is not just a warm fuzzy feeling; it takes making a decision to love a person. It's a love that does not give up on people, no matter how much they disappoint you. Love endures in marriages when a spouse puts on weight or the frown lines and wrinkles start to appear; love still remains and gets stronger with time. Love is when your spouse is sick but you hang in there, and you care for him and support him. Love is being humble even when you know in your heart that you are right about a situation, but you digress to keep confusion down. Love is being kind even when the cashier in the store has a bad attitude. You still show compassion because behind that attitude, she may be going through a terrible situation, and your smile or kindness can brighten her day.

Love does not envy the blessings of others; instead, love rejoices with them. Be happy for others and not envious or jealous, rejoice! Here's one that we deal with a lot today: being overly sensitive or easily provoked. In today's world, you have to be very careful about the words that you say because they can very easily be taken the wrong way. One word is all it takes. Road rage leads to senseless violence and sometimes killings due to stress and frustration. I often see people in the grocery line angry and being disrespectful because the line is not moving fast enough. It's so sad that some people are living life in full-throttle mode, and any interruption or pause will cause them to lose it. The stresses of life can cause some people to be impatient, unloving, and just mean. The love of God is needed much today, but the Bible tells in Matthew 24:12 that because of lawlessness, the love of many will grow cold. This is one of the signs of the end times. We can look at the news or even just the world around us and see love growing colder and colder.

Godly love compels us to see the good in people. It may be hard to see it sometimes, but ask God for His eyes to see them as He sees them. Continue to encourage and pray God's promises for them. Love endures all things—not some, not just what we choose to endure, but *all* things. Love encourages, inspires hope, and builds up. Godly love requires deciding what is good for others and resolving in your heart and mind to do it. You have to be selfless, not self-centered, self-absorbed, nor self-seeking. We cannot be so preoccupied with ourselves that we miss opportunities to display godly love to people. This takes an abandoning of ourselves to do the will of the Father, which is to walk in love (Eph. 5:2). We must reveal the heart of the Father by loving His people. The whole foundation of Jesus coming to earth was out of love for us. His ministry of healings, feeding the hungry, preaching, teaching, and deliverance was because of His love for His people. This is the same love that we must have. The only way that we are able to give this great love is to receive it from Him. We can't give what we do not have. It must come from above, and when we open our hearts to receive from His heart, we are able to have godly love for others.

If there is one thing that you should never doubt, it is God's love for you. I strongly urge you, if you haven't had a true revelation of His love, to receive His love for you now. When we have a true revelation of God's love and grace, it compels us to love Him more and in loving Him, we want to please Him and allow Him into every aspect of our lives. It will change your life forever. It doesn't matter what you've done, He loves you. Don't get caught up in condemnation, shame, guilt, or unworthiness. Don't waste time in that miserable space. Receive this in your spirit,

> For I am persuaded that neither death nor life, nor angels, nor principalities, nor powers, nor things present nor things to come, nor height nor depth, nor any other thing, shall be able to separate me from the love of God which is in Christ Jesus our Lord. (Rom. 8:38–39)

Read this scripture again; breathe in and receive the magnificent, unfailing, divine love of God. He loves you, and there is nothing you can do or cannot do to stop Him from loving you. He just does.

Prayer Matter

Father, I thank You for loving me so much that You gave Your only begotten Son. I receive Your love today. I pray I have a personal revelation of Your divine love for me. I thank You for Your infinite grace and mercy, Lord. No matter what I have done, You still love me. You know my heart, my secret thoughts, and you still love me the same. I thank You for washing away my past, and I no longer have to be bound by feelings of shame. I glorify You, Lord, nothing can separate me from Your love. (Rom. 8:38, 39)

Lord, enable me to have that same kind of love for others. Help me to not give up on people quickly when they disappoint me or when they don't live up to my expectations. Enable me to show mercy and compassion. Show me people whom I need to forgive, and enable me by Your Spirit to forgive them. Eliminate any hard or bad feelings that I may have for them. I ask that You would help me to forgive them by faith.

Where I have been uncaring, unkind, and unloving, Lord, I ask you to forgive me and release into me Your loving kindness. Set me free from anger, envy, impatience, and being overly sensitive. Give me endurance to be long-suffering with others. When I want to give up on someone whom You have ordained to be in my life, give me strength not to give up on them. However, show me those whom I need to totally release into Your hands. Give me special faith for the downtrodden and for people whom others have given up on. Use me as a vessel to show them Your unfailing love through words, deeds, encouragement, and prayer.

Lord when it's all done, I just want You to be able to say, "Well done, my good and faithful servant" (Matt. 25:21). I love you, because You first loved me (1 John 4:19). Thank You for Your unconditional love that was made manifest in Your precious, Son. In Jesus's name, amen.

STRENGTH IN
DIFFICULT TIMES

*God is our refuge and strength, a very present help in
trouble.*

—Psalms 46:1

When going through rough times, I often think about a special friend of mine who has endured and still continues to persevere in spite of very difficult circumstances. She is small in stature but has the spiritual strength of a mighty warrior. She is a vessel full of glory and power of the Almighty God. In spite of her circumstances and challenges, she still remains strong and at peace, and she is full of integrity and unwavering faith. She has kept the faith in times of tragedy, loss, sickness, and caring for a precious loved one. Through it all, she manages to keep a smile on her face.

Prayer Matters

I often wonder how she remains strong despite her circumstances. I know the joy of the Lord is her strength and that it is the Lord keeping her, but how do you get to that place of absolute trust in the Lord? When the turbulence in her life gets overwhelming, how does she remain steady, calm, and at peace? I haven't been through nearly half of the difficulties that she has experienced in life, and at times of what seem like small adversities compared to hers, I feel like I failed the tests. What is even so amazing about my friend, this tower of colossal strength, is that she considers me. When all I want to do is be a blessing to her, pray for her, encourage her, she has a heart to pray for me, encourage me, and be a blessing to me. How could someone who seems to have the weight of the world on her shoulders have an inclination to pray for me? In those times, I have feelings of guilt and inadequacy, but I'm also awed by her selflessness. I'm also encouraged by my friend; she is not easily moved, and I admire that about her. I'm encouraged; if she can get through her difficult times with courage, strength, and perseverance, then so can I! To sum it up, my friend believes God, no matter what.

My friend's determination to make somebody else's life better while she is going through adversity is how I believe God wants all of His children to be. It helps to get your mind off of yourself and be a blessing to others. I came to understand that while blessing others, you in turn are being blessed. You are blessed with strength, endurance, and a heart of gratitude and appreciation. It never fails: every time God leads me to bless someone, I get blessed even more. I'm not doing it to get the blessing, I'm just always blessed when I set out to make somebody's day better. That's how it works when you do things for God. God is so amazing and so marvelously strategic. The measure you give it will be given back to you (Luke 6:38). Even though your intention is not to receive anything, God always gives you a special gift in return, a gift that's placed in your heart. It's hard to describe with mere words. It's a feeling so peaceful and so glorious, and you know in that moment that God orchestrated it all.

God-given strength encourages you to keep moving forward in an attitude of faith, knowing that you can make it because Immanuel (in Hebrew, "God with us") is with us, a very present help in times of trouble (Ps. 46:1). Furthermore, whatever challenges we may be going through, unfortunately somebody, somewhere, is going through worse, and they may be handling it with integrity, without complaining, and without worry. They're not talking to everybody about it over and over again. They're not losing sleep and getting stress headaches. I'm guilty of being up at night, my mind racing, worried about this person or that situation. I feel all this panic while my husband is sleeping peacefully with no worries. When he says he's giving it to God, he gives it God, and he goes to sleep almost instantly.

One night we got a frantic phone call from one of our daughters. She was distraught about some things that were going in on in her life, and she was quite overwhelmed. I was on the phone attempting to calm her down and trying my best to convince her that things were not as bad as she thought, that everything would be OK. I tried my best to reassure her, but nothing seemed to work. At one point in the conversation, I was at a loss for words, overwhelmed and feeling her pain. I reached over and gave the phone to my husband. He talked to our daughter, gave her fatherly words of wisdom, and reassured her that everything was going to be all right. He was practical, nothing deep. Me, I'm known by my kids for always giving mini-sermons and scriptures. This aggravates them at times because it might be a simple question or concern and then there I go with a long-winded message. Well, my daughter calmed down and was encouraged by her father, and it didn't take a speech; it was quite quick. Something about a father can make a daughter feel loved, protected, and assured that everything is going to be OK. I'm sure what he told her was very similar to what I had just told her, but coming from her father, she felt assured, relieved, and comforted, and she had a brand new outlook on her situation. It's like that with our Heavenly Father; when go to Him in prayer and communicate our hurts and needs, He comforts us like no one else can. We have the assurance in knowing that everything will be all right.

Moving forward, my husband and daughter ended the phone conversation. It wasn't two minutes after my husband hung up the phone that I heard him snoring, I couldn't believe it. I mean, he was asleep in a split second. Me, oh, I was up all night worrying if she was really going to be OK. Oh, and I also did some "worry praying"—you know, worrying and praying at the same time. Instead, I should have prayed, released my daughter and the situation to God, trusted Him, and went to sleep like my husband. I should have made a decision to trust God and be at rest. It's weird how we know what to do, but in times of distress, we miss the mark sometimes. If we are not careful, we panic, get emotional, and before you know it, we can work ourselves up into a frenzy. We must be mindful to take a moment stop and pray in faith, believing that God will answer and that He is moving on your behalf, no matter the trial.

When I think of someone who had to endure a lot of suffering and trials, I think of Job. In the book of Job, we are introduced to a man who is blameless and upright, and he fears the Lord (Job 1:1). In fact, in Job 1:3, it says that Job is the greatest of all the people of the East. Job seems to have it all. He has an excellent family that consists of a wife, seven sons, and three daughters. Also, he has great wealth and possessions. Yes, Job is abundantly blessed and prosperous. That is until Satan questions Job's character. So Satan says to the Lord,

Does not Job fear God for nothing? Have You not made a hedge of protection around him, around his household, and around all that he has on every side? You have blessed the work of his hands, and his possessions have increased in the land. (Job 9–10)

Satan is questioning Job's motives for why he is serving God. Job has it all. Is this why he is such an upright man, for protection and possessions? Is this Job's incentive for serving the Lord? Satan attacks Job's character and says to God to "stretch out His hand and touch all that he has, and he will surely curse You to your face" (Job 1:11)! In so many words, Satan is saying, Job is only serving God for stuff, and if you take his stuff away from him, he won't serve God anymore; in fact, he will curse Him!"

God allows for Satan to take Job's possessions, children, and his health, but he cannot take his life (Job 1:12). All of Job's losses happen in one day. In one day, his life is dramatically and drastically changed. Think of the excruciating emotional pain, sorrow, devastation, agony, and anguish he must've experienced. After the loss of his children and all that he owns, he worships God and says, "Naked I came from my mother's womb, and naked shall I return there. The Lord gave, and the Lord has taken away; Blessed be the name of the Lord" (Job 1:21). In the midst of all of the suffering, Job worships and recognizes God as sovereign and knows that He is in control (Job 1:21). Then, to make matters worse, he is also stricken with painful boils from the soles of his feet to the crown of his head. His pain has to be excruciating and unbearable, and he scrapes himself (Job 2:7–9). He is in both extreme emotional pain and agonizing physical pain. If ever you would think, "It can't really get any worse than this," this would be the time, and I would say it would be a very legitimate statement under Job's circumstances. Then, to add insult to injury, Job's wife is not supportive or a source of encouragement. She says to him, "Do you still hold fast to your integrity? Curse God and die!" Talk about kicking you while you are down. If anybody should have your back and give you support, it should be your spouse. I'm sure his wife was devastated; what he lost, she also lost—her children, home, everything. But Job remains faithful to God and responds to her, "Shall we indeed accept good from God, and shall we not

Prayer Matters

accept adversity? In all this Job did not sin with his lips" (Job 2:10). Although God is not bringing about these calamities to happen, Job believes that God is the cause, and yet he has complete trust in God and he accepts the good and the bad. Job accepts God's will. In our own lives, things may not turn out the way we'd like or even the way we prayed. Ultimately, it's God's will that will be done, and we have to learn to accept His will in every situation. Sometimes in His will there will be hard things that we have to go through. We may not understand why we have to go through certain situations, but we have to trust in God and His sovereignty and trust that He is working out a greater purpose in the situation. We must trust that no matter how bad it is, He will get the glory out of it, and we will come out stronger and blessed on the other side of our trials.

God permits Job to be tested by Satan, but He knows who is taking the test. During his test, Job has an array of emotions and challenges. His friends believe that he has done something wrong to deserve all the troubles that have befallen him. Although they have good intentions to comfort and console him, they are not a comfort to him at all. In fact, Job calls them "miserable comforters" (Job 16:1). I can relate to that; sometimes people mean well, but they only seem to make things worse by saying the wrong things. They might also have a distorted view of what is really going on. That is why it is beneficial to always seek the mind of God in situations before trying to give advice or comfort to others. I've done it out of nervousness or not knowing what to say to someone who was in distress. In addition to that, sometimes people who are going through tough times are more sensitive and can be easily offended because of their fragile states. Even something like giving a scripture at the wrong time could create trouble. For example, "My brethren, count it all joy when you fall into various trials" (James 1:2). This is a very powerful scripture, but I don't think this would be a comfort to most when they are at their darkest times. Being led by the Holy Spirit is very important. We never want to be what Job called his friends: "miserable comforters."

God knows who is taking the test, just as he knows us when we are facing trials. Job begins to have feelings that I've felt and that I'm sure we all have felt some time or another. In Job 10:7, Job says, "You know that I am not wicked." Some may feel the same way: "Lord I love you, I try to live a righteous life a life that is pleasing to You, so why is this happening to me?" In Job 10:18, Job even asks, "Why have you brought me out of the womb? Oh, that I had perished and no eye had seen me! I would have been as though I had not been. I would have been carried from the womb to the grave." Job feels sorry for himself. I've been invited to and have hosted a few pity parties myself. You cry, "Woe is me, why is God allowing this to happen to me?" When going through a trial sometimes it can be quite easy to start murmuring, complaining, and feeling sorry for yourself. The pity parties are not fun, but for some reason, at times I've felt like I just wanted to stay in those dark places. It didn't feel good, but I just wanted to feel sorry for myself and have other people feel sorry for me as well. Instead of overcoming, I succumbed to being the victim. Why me, Lord? That's why it's great to have those friends who encourage you in the Lord, those friends who pray you through and reassure you that God is in control and that "He's got you, girl!" No miserable comforters—we need comforters who are believers and who encourage you in the Lord.

"Though He slay me, yet I will trust Him" (Job 13:15). Job thinks that God will eventually take his life, and yet he trusts God. Job trusts God, but he also pleads his case to Him. He says, "Why do you hide Your face, and regard me as Your enemy?" (Job 13:24).

Have you ever felt like God has hid His face from you? Have you ever thought, "God, where are you?" You know He's real, but in the midst of your dark situation, you can't see Him. He doesn't seem to be answering your prayers. What have I done to deserve this?

Prayer Matters

Job knows the feeling. Job complains and even questions God. Job wants to know what had he done to deserve all of the devastating things happening to him. I confess that I've had those feelings in seasons of testing. As much as I wanted to stay strong and keep the faith, at times I felt that I had failed the test with a big fat "F." It's like you know what to do, you pray, believe as much as you can, and meditate on His promises, but you feel like your efforts are not moving the hand of God, and things just don't seem to be getting better or not fast enough. When will it be over? You try your best to persevere, but you get weary and discouraged. You try to stay in a position of faith, but if we are not alert and prayerful, our faith can start to waver, and doubt can creep in. This is the time when we really have to pray for endurance.

Job endures but not always with the best attitude. I confess I've been guilty of not having the best attitude when I'm under stress. One day I'd feel like I was strong and could conquer the world, the devil is under my feet. The next day I'd be feeling sorry for myself. Job seems to be having this roller-coaster of feelings, but overall he trusts in the sovereignty of God. When he is in doubt of God's being in control, God reveals Himself to Job in a whirlwind (Job 38:1)! That alone has to put Job in his place, a place of reverence and submission to God Almighty! Then God says to Job, "Now prepare yourself like a man; I will question you, and you shall answer Me" (Job 38:3). Can you imagine that? It reminds me of getting in trouble when I was a teenager. My mom said, "You want to be grown; I'm going to treat you like you're grown." God tells Job to prepare yourself like a man. Job has all these questions for God. Now God had questions for Him. I would not have wanted to be in Job's position at that time, answering God's questions. God emphasizes to Job His control over everything, from creating the universe and everything in it to Him putting wisdom in the mind and understanding in the heart (Job 38). Further, in chapter 39, God challenges Job and confronts him. God says to Job,

Have you an arm like God? Or can you thunder a voice like His? Then adorn yourself with majesty and splendor, and array yourself with glory and beauty. Disperse the rage of your wrath; Look on everyone who is proud, and humble him. (Job 39:9–11)

God is letting Job know who He is, and who Job is not.

God goes on to say that, "Everything under heaven is mine" (Job 41:11). I'm sure this was a humbling experience for Job, to say the least. This reminds me of the speech I got from my mom once. "Do you pay any bills in this house? I pay the cost to be the boss!" In other words, who do you think you are? You have no authority, so get and stay in your lane. After Job's dialogue with God, his attitude begins to change. Whose wouldn't after an encounter with The Most High God?

In Job 42:1–3, Job responds to God by saying,

I know that You can do everything, and that no purpose of Yours can be withheld from You. You asked, 'Who is this who hides counsel without knowledge?' Therefore, I have uttered what I did not understand, things too wonderful for me, which I did not know.

Job knows that God can do everything. Although he doesn't understand his sufferings, He now knows that God has a purpose, and it was God's will that had to be done. Job repents and confesses that God's plans are too wonderful for him to comprehend. Job goes on to say that, "I have heard of You by the hearing of the ear, but now my eye sees You" (Job 42:5). Job had heard, but now he sees and experiences God for himself. It's just like us having head knowledge; we can know the word of God and hear the word of God, but God has to open our spiritual eyes of understanding for us to really see. We also have

Prayer Matters

to experience Him. This often comes from going through trials. I would not have experienced God as my Healer if I had not been sick. I would not know God to be my Deliverer if He hadn't delivered me. When you see God heal you, see Him provide for you, see Him save your child, see Him protect you, it uplifts your faith! You might've read about God, but now, like Job, your eyes see! If you didn't know, now you know! You no longer have to go by what someone told you; you can see God's glory and faithfulness for yourself!

God restores Job and He will restore you too! The Lord gives Job twice as much as he had before. He restores his family by giving him seven sons and three daughters. He restores his wealth and prosperity. God restores Job's health and he lives one hundred and forty years and he sees his children and grandchildren for four generations! (Job 10–17) God knew who was taking the test. God knew that Job would remain faithful. He also knew how much Job could take. He knows you, He knows who is taking the test, He knows how much you can withstand. He knows you can endure because He is with you. You may not understand His purpose, but His plan is so wondrous, our minds cannot conceive it. Stand on His promises, keep the faith no matter how bad it seems, and God will carry you through, just place absolute trust in Him. Trust in His sovereignty, for He is in control. Who better to be in control but God? He is working out a greater, everlasting purpose. Know that He is with you, and you are never alone. He will restore and carry out His awesome plan for your life.

The only way that we can have strength to withstand difficult times is in God. Abide in Him, believe Him, and take Him at His word. He is our Strength and our Refuge. Whatever the problem, find out what God says about it in His Word, and get in agreement with Him. There is a restful place where you can abide in Him, a place of absolute assurance in knowing that He is working it all out for your good because He loves and cares for you. That place is found by seeking His heart in total and complete surrender of every area of your life to Him. Surrender all to receive all. Through faith and patience, we receive the promises, and He never breaks a promise (Heb. 6:12). Be encouraged and pray, believe, and wait for the promises of God: "For all the promises of God in Him are Yes, and in Him Amen, to the glory of God through us" (2 Cor. 1:20).

Prayer Matter
Father, in the name of Jesus, I thank You that even in the darkest of times, You are with me. You are Immanuel God with me. You never leave me or forsake me (Deut. 31:6). I thank You for loving me with an everlasting love (Jer. 31:3). You are my Everlasting Father, and you care for me. You care about my situation and how I feel. Help me not to lean on my own understanding but in all my ways acknowledge You, and You will direct my paths (Prov. 3:5). I ask You to enable me to release my problem, my trial, my spouse, my children, our health, and our lives to You by faith, surrendering everything to You, Your will be done. Although at times I don't understand, I know that You are working out such a greater purpose. I trust You, Lord.

Lord, give me assurance to know that everything is going to be all right. Help me to find rest in your arms. I don't want to worry, Lord, but I still find myself worrying about things that I have no control over. Enable me to release these things into Your hands and leave them there. Only You can restore and bring consolation and everlasting hope into my life. Lord, where I have been burdened down by worry, anxiety, and stress, I ask You to forgive me and free me from these tormenting emotions. I receive Your all-sufficient grace. I thank You, for Your strength is made perfect in my weakness (2 Cor. 12:9). Bring me to a place of rest and peace that can only be found in You.

You are Jehovah Shalom (The Lord is Peace), and I pray that You will grant me peace. I know that it's OK to have concern, but it's not OK to worry. For Your Word says, "Don't worry about my life" (Matt. 6:1). Bring me to a place of abiding in You where there is rest for my soul, a place of

Prayer Matters

comfort and absolute assurance and confidence that You have me right where You want me to be—close to You. With You, I know that I triumph! I trust and believe in You, no matter what my eyes may see. I know that You are working out something remarkable in and for me. In You alone I put my trust. In Jesus's name I pray, amen.

ALTOGETHER BEAUTIFUL

You are altogether beautiful, my love, there is no flaw in you.

—Song of Solomon 4:7

How do you perceive yourself? When you look in the mirror, what is the first thought that comes into your mind? When you look at yourself, do you notice all the imperfections, the things that you don't like about yourself? Or maybe you criticize your body, resolving that you have too much of this and not enough of that. You wish that your nose was slimmer, your eyes wider. Your hair texture is too straight, too kinky, or too frizzy. You may not even like to look in the mirror. On the other hand, you may have the tendency to look in the mirror too much. For some, it may not be superficial. They may see the hurt little girl in the mirror, the little girl who was molested, all her innocence taken away. It's hard for her to look at

Prayer Matters

herself. She feels dirty and ashamed, like everything that was once pure is gone, taken away from her against her will. The little girl whose father abandoned her still feels the emptiness in her heart. She's given her heart to many men, and yet her heart is hollow inside.

The former you and your former experiences can shape how you feel about yourself today and how you allow yourself to be treated by others. They affect your relationships, how you view life, how you view yourself, and how you view other people.

I want you to know and receive in your heart that you are altogether beautiful—yes, you. That means that everything about you is lovely. There is no flaw in you, no defect (Solomon 4:7). However your nose is shaped, whatever size you are, whatever handicap or disability, you are lovely. I don't care if you were sexually abused, verbally abused, abandoned, teased—I want you to know that you are altogether beautiful. You are God's priceless, perfect design, and there is no one else like you. You are special, valuable, and loved by the One who created you, and He loves you with an everlasting love. From the outside to your inner parts, you are fearfully and wonderfully made, and you have worth and value. You were crafted by God Almighty, the Master, the Creator! When we get a real revelation of who God is, we can have a greater understanding and appreciation for who we are, and we can know that our worth cannot be measured by human understanding. As you get to know Him, the more you will love Him, and the more you will love who He created, you. As you start to have a personal relationship with Him, you'll start to see the family likeness, and as you transform into His image, you will begin to set standards for yourself as to how you will allow yourself to be treated and how you treat yourself and others. God wants His best for you, and He wants you to desire it also. He wants us not to settle for less when what He has is so much greater. Insecurity and low self-esteem can come from past experiences or the world's standards that cause us to have wrong perceptions of ourselves. What's needed is a God-eyed view of ourselves. How does God see us?

First, in the beginning of mankind, God creates man in His likeness: "So God created man in His own image; in the image of God He created him; male and female He created them" (Gen. 1:27). God sees that everything He made is very good, including the male and female whom He creates in His likeness. Not almost good, or somewhat good, but very good, including you (Gen. 1:31). See, we are created in His image, so His characteristics and attributes are to be manifested in us. Although we have a sinful nature because of Adam and Eve's disobedience, as we get to know and submit to God, we begin to take on more of His nature. We start to reflect Him more and more. Once we begin to start seeking God's heart, He reveals to us who He is, and we can better understand who He created us to be. All of who we are is in relationship to Jesus. Only in Jesus is our true intended identity.

As we seek God and abide in Him, there will be a shift in how we perceive ourselves. What people think about you won't be so important anymore. The value you put on yourself will not come from what you look like, bad past experiences, how you were brought up, or how much money you have. Your worth will not come from what people say or have said about you. You will know that your worth comes from God. When you know who you are in Christ, people's opinions about you won't matter. The need to fit in won't be so important anymore. You won't compare yourself to others. Your whole purpose will be to please God. You will move from a superficial perspective to a spiritual perspective. Temporal issues won't be so pressing anymore; you will have a more eternal way of thinking.

So many women, including me, have allowed what society or devastating things in their past dictate their present and their futures. In the past, I have allowed myself to be treated horribly by men and by people in general because I had no idea of how valuable I was. I wanted to be loved so much so that I allowed myself to be disrespected in relationships that were not healthy for me, relationships that God never intended for me to be in. I've been married a long time, but I kissed a couple of frogs before I found my "king."

As I reflect back, I had no idea of who I was because I didn't know God. All I knew is that I wanted so desperately to feel loved. A lot of the relationship examples that I had seen were not healthy ones. So, in comparison, I thought my relationships were not that bad. To be honest, as I reflect back, I was desperate for love. I think it had a lot to do with my parents divorcing and my father leaving the house. Although my dad has never left my life, deep down I felt that he abandoned his "old" family for a "better," new family. When my dad started his "new" family and got remarried, this made me have feelings of not being good enough. I now know that wasn't the case, but as a kid, that's how I felt. My parents' divorce and the breakup of our family left an emptiness inside of me. The emptiness I felt caused me to seek love and attention in unhealthy relationships. I had two very unhealthy relationships before I married my husband. In both relationships, I was cheated on, lied to, and mistreated. I didn't think enough of myself to get out of these bad relationships. I accepted imitation love. I felt a little of something was better than a lot of nothing. I was taking what I could get, which was not much. I knew in my heart that the treatment that I was receiving in those relationships was not right. I settled and took the good with the bad. The bad outnumbered the good, and I still hung in there. The relationships that I thought would fill that hole in my heart only made the hole deeper.

You see where I set the bar for myself is how I was treated. I'm a firm believer that you have to set the bar high. If your standards are set low regarding how you will be treated, that is what you will attract, and that is how you will be treated—with low regard. I was only treated like garbage because I allowed it. If I knew who I was in God, I would have seen "Mr. Smooth" and "Mr. No Good" coming from a mile away and wouldn't have given them the time of day. It's hard to admit, but the only way those relationships were broken off is because they were the ones who broke them off. Sad, isn't it? I know God was watching over me even then. I didn't have the strength or sense to stop the madness, but God allowed for me not to continue to be hurt and abused. The breakups hurt badly, and I thought that I would never get over them at the time. But boy, as I look back and reflect on how my life could have turned out, I praise God for looking out for me even then.

That is why it is so important to know God, pray about your mate, set standards, and to know what attributes a godly man has—a man who knows, loves, and walks with Jesus and who shows true godly character. If you are not married, then I urge you to wait on God and His best for you. It will save you a lot of heartache, embarrassment, shame, and time. It all goes back to setting our eyes on our Father, seeking Him first, and all things shall be added unto you in His timing. He must be the Love of your life first and foremost. God wants your whole heart first, then you will be able to share it with the man that he has for you. There is a place in your heart for God, and no man and nothing can fill it until He's allowed total residency. When God has your whole heart, you will be more willing to wait for His best you. You will be able to discern a true man of God and not one just perpetrating to be one. If God truly has your heart, you won't settle, because you know that God has something better in store for you. I could have saved myself a lot of turmoil from looking for love in all the obviously wrong places, if I had instead been seeking God, the lover of my soul, who loves me like no other. By abiding in His love, you get an accurate perception of who you are—His love manifested, altogether beautiful.

Most of my life, I've had both a poor self-image and body image. My poor body image started as a young girl going through premature puberty. Not only was I developing early, but it seemed to me to be instantly and at an accelerated pace. At first, it didn't bother me that much, but when the boys started to take notice, it made me very uncomfortable—to say the least. They stared, made remarks, and tried to inappropriately touch me. When I was walking home from school, older men would stare and make comments. This made me resent my body even more. I was never satisfied with the way I looked; I always thought I was fat. As I look back at some of my old teenage pictures, I think to myself, "You were a bad mamma-jamma." I can laugh at it now, but it's also sad at the same time. I look back and think, I was something pretty special and didn't even know it. God looks at us the same way. He knows that we are something special, lovely, fearfully and wonderfully made, and some don't even know it.

There are so many self-help books that tackle "self," and low self-esteem. The issue of self-love and low self-esteem still arises, even in these days of people taking countless "selfies" of themselves. The world's understanding of self-esteem is how you feel you are valued by your accomplishments, how you look, how much money you have, and your title or position. It's based on temporary, superficial things that have no eternal value. Having a healthy self-image comes from our relationship with God. Too much esteem, both low or high, is a form of pride and is self-centered. Our lives should be God-centered. Psalms 16:2 says, "O my soul, You have said to the Lord, You are my God, my goodness is nothing apart from You." Everything good that is in us is from the Lord. How can I boast about anything? The goodness that I have is from God; nothing in me apart from God is good because He gives me the goodness. All that is within us is to give Him glory through giving our gifts, loving others, and ministering to others' needs: "Therefore as it is written, He who glories, let him glory in the Lord" (1 Cor. 1:31). God be glorified, in us and through us. In all our goals, our first and most important goal must be seeking first His kingdom and His righteousness (Matt. 6:33).

"For I say, through the grace given to me, to everyone who is among you, not to think of himself more highly than he ought to think, but to think soberly, as God has dealt to each one a measure of faith" (Rom. 12:3). Thinking too highly of ourselves is dangerous, and it can cause people to idolize themselves. They get puffed up with pride, and God is not pleased with that behavior. It happens in the secular world and sadly sometimes in the church. People are into titles and positions, which are fine if they come from God and are received and carried out in humility. Jesus is our example of true humility and service. When the disciples argue about who is the greatest among them, Jesus says to them, "For who is greater, he who sits at the table, or he who serves? Is it not he who sits at the table? Yet I am among you as the One who serves." Jesus's view of greatness is the opposite of the world's perspective. Jesus is the Great I Am, yet He humbles Himself as a mere man, to serve, not to be served, and to give His life a ransom for many (Mark 11:45).

However, having too low of an opinion of oneself is not healthy, either. When God tells Moses that He is going to send him to Pharaoh to bring the children out of Egypt, Moses is reluctant, to say the least. He doesn't feel adequate or worthy. Moses says in Exodus 3:11, "Who am I that I should go to Pharaoh, and that I should bring the children of Israel out of Egypt?" God reassures Moses that he will certainly be with him, but Moses is still hesitant and asks God, "Indeed when I come to the children of Israel and say to them, 'The God of your fathers has sent me to you,' and they say to me, 'What is His name?' What shall I say to them?" And God says to Moses, "I AM WHO I AM" (Exod. 3:12–14). Moses goes even further in Exodus 4:10: "Then Moses said to the Lord, 'O my Lord, I am not eloquent, neither before nor since You have spoken to Your servant, but I am slow of speech and tongue.' The Lord reassured Moses and said to Him, 'Who has made man's mouth?'" (Exod. 4:11). God reassures Moses again, "'Now therefore, go, and I will be with your mouth and teach you what you shall say.' But he said, 'O my Lord, please send by the hand of whomever else You may send'" (Exod. 4:12–13). God is being patient with Moses up until this point. I mean, this is God Almighty sending him on

Prayer Matters

an assignment and Moses keeps making excuses. So the anger of the Lord is kindled against Moses, and God sends Aaron, Moses's brother, to assist Moses. Moses is to speak to Aaron what God spoke to him. Aaron becomes Moses's spokesperson.

Like Moses, at times I too have insecurities. I feel inadequate and sometimes fearful. When I know that God is telling me to do something, these feeling often creep in. I worry about what I'm going to say. What if I say the wrong thing? Did I pray the right way? There have been many times when I have been asked to do things in ministry and have let fear stop me. Sometimes I feel like I'm not good enough or equipped enough. I'd often, like Moses, feel like, "O my Lord, please send someone else, how about Sister So-and-So, she's a great speaker and she loves to talk. How about Brother Wails, he's is a great prayer warrior and he can get a prayer through." God is patient, but I would not want His anger to be kindled toward me like it was with Moses. God has an assignment for Moses, and He has one for you me and you. Every day we are on an assignment from God. Like with a homework assignment, you have to read, study, and follow the directions that the teacher gives you. To know your godly assignment, you have to read and study the Bible, follow the instructions in it, and follow God's leading for direction.

Like with Moses, God is with you, and He will teach you what to say.

Moses has to be assured by God that He is with him. Moses is obedient and goes to Egypt, encounters Pharaoh, and through his obedience God demonstrates His power by doing many signs and wonders through him. God parts the Red Sea. Thus, the Israelites are free from slavery through Moses finally getting over his insecurities.

God can work mightily through you as well. It takes having an active faith and trusting in God. Not in who you are, not in your abilities, not in your strength, but in who God is and His all-powerful

145

abilities. Harboring feelings of not being good enough is not a good enough excuse for you to not to allow God to use you. All you have to do is just be a willing vessel for Him to use. Allow God to work through you. He knows your frame (Ps. 103:13). He created you and knows all about you. Every insecurity that you have can be secure in Him if you just allow Him to complete His good work in you (Phil. 1:6). It's not so much as having self-confidence but putting confidence in Him, a complete trust and dependence on Him to work out and do in you what you cannot do on your own: "Such confidence we have through Christ before God. Not that we are competent in ourselves to claim anything for ourselves, but our competence comes from God" (2 Cor. 3:4–5).

Being humble and being insecure are two different things. Humility doesn't mean thinking that you're not good enough or letting people walk all over you. Humility is understanding who you are in relationship to God. You know that your flesh is inadequate, but in Christ you are adequate. It's knowing that in yourself you can do nothing, but in Christ you can do all things through Him who strengthens you (Phil. 4:13). It all must come from Him, nothing in ourselves. A total dependence upon Him means humbling yourself before Him. It means never seeking self-will but God's will, for His glory, not ours. Humility is not being weak but being strong in the Lord and His strength.

Only in Him are we strong, confident, and secure. It does not matter if someone told you that you wouldn't ever amount to anything. Someone may have called you ugly, fat, stupid, or "You're just like your father." Seek in God's Word who He is and who He says you are; that is what is true about you. Believe it! Put on the new man, which was created according to God, in true righteousness and holiness (Eph. 4:24). You may look in the mirror, and you might not see it right now. When you look in the mirror, you might still see the hurt little girl or the promiscuous teenager. Just believe that the more that you abide in God and get to know Him, you are looking like Him more and more. "But we all, with unveiled face, beholding as in a mirror the glory of the Lord, are being transformed into the same image from glory to glory, just as by the Spirit of the Lord." (2 Cor. 3:18) Yes, as you behold the glory of the Lord in the Word of God and apply it to your life, you will be transformed into His image and likeness! From glory to glory! Altogether beautiful!

Prayer Matter

Father, I come to You, giving thanks for all that You are. You are the Creator of all mankind, and I thank you for making and molding me in Your likeness. You personally sculpted every intricate part of me, and I am Your unique masterpiece. You know everything about me; You tell me in Your Word, "But the very hairs of your head are all numbered. Do not fear therefore; you are of more value than many sparrows" (Luke 12:6). I thank You for loving me with an everlasting love, a love that never ends. I thank You for loving me so much that You gave Your Only Son so that I may have everlasting life (John 3:16). I'm forever grateful to You for giving Your Precious Perfect Son. Though He is without sin, spot, or blemish. Thank you for the Gift that You have given me. I know that I have worth and value because of the redemptive work of Jesus. I'm forever grateful and thankful.

Free me from myself, from all self-absorption, selfish motives, selfish desires, and self-centeredness. I know that too much introspection and being overly concerned about what I look like or what I want is a form of pride and is vanity. Help me to be more concerned about my spiritual life and what You want to do through me. Create in me a strong desire for more of You, Your Word, Your Way, and Your Presence. I know that You want all my heart, my soul, my mind, and my life. Reveal to me any areas in my life that I have not totally surrendered to You, and help me to relinquish those areas to You. I ask you to heal me from past hurtful relationships. Bind up all emotional wounds of verbal, emotional, physical, and sexual abuse. Restore me and make me whole in You.

Where there are any idols in my life, I pray that You will tear them down. Whether those idols are things, people, or me, Lord, may I put You in Your rightful place on the throne of my heart. May I long to be in Holy Communion with You. In Your presence, I abide in You and get to know You. In getting to know You, I have a true revelation of who I am—not as the world would have me to be, but who You purposed for me to be. May You take precedence over everything and everybody in my life. Set me free from people pleasing, wanting to fit in, and from competing and comparing myself to others. Help me to love and accept the person whom You created me to be. Father, help me to only believe what You say about me. You say that I am fearfully and wonderfully made (Ps. 139:14). Help me to turn away my eyes from looking at vanity, and revive me in Your ways (Ps. 119:37 ASV).

Lord, I ask You to heal me of the hurtful words spoken to me or about me. Where I have been violated in any way, help me to forgive and be able to move forward with my life. I am not that same hurt little girl, the misfit, the violated one, the ugly one. I am a child of the King, the Most High. I am the apple of Your eye (Ps. 17:8). Nothing superficial will satisfy the longing in my heart. I will worship you in the beauty of Your holiness, and that is where true beauty is. You are glorious. In Your presence, I am adorned with purity, love, and holiness. I am embellished by Your Spirit and Your beauty. In Jesus's name, I pray and give thanks, amen.

RUNNING ON EMPTY

I will refresh the weary and satisfy the faint.

—Jeremiah 31:25

Have you ever had times of just plain exhaustion? Do you ever feel just tired, worn out, weary, and frustrated? Your days are running together, and you can hardly remember when they start and when they end. The alarm clock goes off, and you hit the snooze button—maybe even a couple of times. You finally get up, and your mind starts to race with thoughts of all the things you have to do that day. The list can go on and on. Yes, our days may vary in activities, but for most of us, it can get quite hectic and overwhelming at times. Our lives seem to mostly revolve around other people: your children, husband, parents, coworkers, and even church. There is nothing wrong with giving of ourselves. That is how we are supposed to be, right? We are saved to serve. Give, and it shall be given to you. Yes, but what happens if you seem to always be giving, and you feel like you have nothing left to give? You are wearing out, burned out, and longing for a vacation on a deserted island somewhere. You feel like that old television commercial: "Calgon, take me away." Well, I'm telling my age—some may not remember that commercial—but you can just imagine. You know those times when all you want at the end of the day is a nice, warm, fragrant bubble bath with candles and some peace and quiet. Just a relaxing time for just you to have stillness of mind and body. But then—there's a knock at the bathroom door. One kid is telling on the other, the phone is ringing, someone is ringing the doorbell, and your husband can't find the remote control. There goes the relaxing bath. Frustration starts to set in, but you get up and do what you have to do, and you try to do it with a good attitude even though you're a bit resentful and deep down a little agitated.

The truth is that you can't give what you don't have. Making time for yourself is most importantly for you to get refreshed, but in the long run, it enables you to help others more effectively. You'll be more energized and your attitude will also improve. Yes, it can be difficult to find "me" time. Depending on your circumstances, it can be hard to find time to nurture yourself. Some may have the responsibility of caring for aging parents in addition to taking care of their own families. Many are caring for children with special needs. Young adults have the pressures of college, working, and uncertainty about their futures. Women have the responsibility of caring for kids, husbands, cleaning, cooking, carpooling, grocery shopping, careers, etc. Single moms have the tremendous task of doing all these things by themselves. There are so many things to do in this fast-paced world that can exhaust us. What do we do when we are running on empty? What do you do when you are drained, and if you try to give any more, you are going to lose it? How do you find the opportunity to regroup, relax, restore, and refresh you?

If you are out of commission or "out of order," then the house is out of order, the kids are out of order, and your life will be out

Prayer Matters

of order. Your life will be in disorder and in dysfunction. So making time for yourself as well as taking good care of yourself is necessary. You have a responsibility to yourself, to God, and to the people who depend on you to take good care of yourself. If you are not good to yourself, you can't be any good to someone else effectively. We as women especially have a tendency to put ourselves last. I know I do. I fix my plate last, eat last, and get the last piece of chicken—usually the piece that I don't like and that no one else wants. We often put our needs aside for others. We could use new shoes, but the kids come first. That movie you may have so desperately wanted to see you didn't see, because your husband wanted to see a new sci-fi flick instead. So you sit through the movie, and you don't even like science-fiction movies, but you grin and bear it. Consider the single mom who planned to finally treat herself to a new hairdo, but had to opt out because she had to pay for her son's upcoming field trip.

Yes, we compromise a lot and put ourselves last. Why? Because we love our family and friends, and we want them to be happy. The word "No" is a two-letter word, but is so hard to say. So you go ahead and do the thing that you don't want to do, and try to do it with a good attitude. Some things we have no choice but to do, like go to work, take care of the kids, be attentive in marriage, housework, church etc. But what are some things on your "to do list" that can be eliminated? Maybe there are even some people who are draining you by not adding anything positive to your life. Instead, they are subtracting your joy, peace, money, and time, and maybe their presence in your life should be minimal or absent entirely. Seek God and He will show you the people who are continually draining you with no intention to help themselves. Those whom you are to pray for and leave the outcome to God.

When you are running on empty, praying, prioritizing, and finding rest in God helps to eliminate a lot of stress, frustration, exhaustion, resentment, and bitterness from your life. I've learned personally for me that it's better to do a few things well than doing a lot of things halfway.

Saturdays are usually set aside for me to do major cleaning in my house. I clean during the week, but Saturdays are when I really dig in. I'll have a list in my mind of all the things that I PLAN to get done. For example, I might start by putting a load of laundry in washer. Then, I run downstairs, attacking the kitchen by starting to wash the dishes in the sink—yes, I still hand wash my dishes. I have a dishwasher that I never use for some reason. In the meantime, the washer goes off, and I run back upstairs to take the clothes out of the washer and put them in the dryer. While I'm upstairs, I start to vacuum. Then the phone rings in my bedroom, so I answer it, and I'm on the phone for twenty minutes. While I'm upstairs, I might as well start disinfecting my bathtub. While cleaning the bathroom, I realize that I forgot to pay a bill. I go to the computer to pay the bill and the password that I use to pay the bill is not working. Then, I spend a half hour trying to figure out the password with no luck. Simultaneously, I start to think about what I'm going to fix for dinner—maybe burgers? Then I run back downstairs to take the meat out of the fridge. I start back on the dishes that I left in the sink, and then I remember that I have to reset my password to pay the bill. In the meantime, my brother's car won't start, so I have to take him to work. I'm getting exhausted just thinking about it.

My scheduled list that I had made in my mind is not going as planned. So what if I didn't get everything done, and my plans went down the drain? "There are many plans in a man's heart, Nevertheless the Lord's counsel-that will stand" (Prov. 19:21). We can plan all we want, but we can't even direct our own steps (Jer. 10:23). When I answered the phone that day I had set out to clean, it was someone who needed encouragement. When I took my brother to work, it was an opportunity to minister to him. When I went to the computer to pay the bill, maybe I just needed to sit

Prayer Matters

down. We are to never be so stuck in own plans that we're not allowing God to move freely through us to do as He wills.

When we become overwhelmed and depleted by life, Jesus gives us the answer in the Word of God. He says, "Come to Me, all who labor and are heavy laden, and I will give you rest. Take My yoke upon you and learn from Me, for I am gentle and lowly in heart, and you will find rest for your souls. For my yoke is easy and My burden is light" (Matt. 11:28–30). In this verse, Jesus is talking to the people whom the Pharisees had burdened with loads of laws and regulations. No one could ever live up to all of the legalistic requirements of the Pharisees. In not being able to do so, the people become heavy laden. Jesus tells them to take His yoke upon them. His yoke is easy and His burden is light. They don't have to try to fulfill the law because Jesus fulfills the Law (Matt. 5:17). He relieves them from their heavy burden, and they can find rest for their souls. Jesus does the same for us today. We have the freedom to go to Jesus when we are overwhelmed and exhausted, and in going to Him and abiding in Him, we get relief from all frustration, exhaustion, anxiety, and burnout. The added bonus is that we get refreshed, refilled, revived, and rejuvenated.

Jesus says to take His yoke upon us, but He also says to learn from Him. Let's see, what can we learn from Jesus through His example about getting alone sometimes and resting?

> Then the apostles gathered to Jesus and told Him all things, both what they had done and what they had taught. And He said to them, "Come aside by yourselves to a deserted place and rest awhile." For there were many coming and going, and they did not even have time to eat. So they departed to a deserted place in the boat by themselves. (Mark 6:30-32)

Jesus cares for His disciples and He directs them to go get some rest in a deserted place because there are so many people. Our lives can be that way sometimes. At times we need to come aside to ourselves and rest awhile in an isolated place, a place where there is just you and God. There is true rest and freedom to be found in God. When you truly rest in Him, you don't worry about the cares of the world. You don't worry about your kids, your husband, the bills, your job, or your life. You release all those things to Him and rest in the comfort of His everlasting arms, knowing that He has everything under control. In that rest, there is uninterrupted, divine peace and a serenity that overtakes you, moment by moment. That place is also refreshing. When you truly rest in God, He replenishes your mind, body, and spirit. You just relax, lay limp in His embracing arms, trust Him to hold you up, and know that He will not let you fall. You have full trust and confidence in Him. In His arms you don't have a care in the world. Things will still be going on around you, but you will have a stillness within you.

As busy as our schedules may get, it is imperative that we get intimate time alone with God. Yes, we love our families and friends, and we are commanded to love all people. But we cannot be effective in what God has called us to do for others unless we take time out to care for ourselves in totality: mind, body, and spirit. I'm a firm believer that what you put in is what you get out. You are what you put into your mind, body, and spirit. And in order to be healthy in every aspect, we have to put in things that will nourish, strengthen, and grow us. We must feed our minds on the Word of God. We must feed, chew, and meditate on the Word of God daily. This strengthens and renews our minds and spirits. How can we stand and believe on God's promises if we don't know them? Determine to know the promises of God and to know His Word. The Word not only transforms your mind to the mind of Christ, but it enables you to bring every thought into captivity to the obedience of Christ (2Cor. 10:5b). Just as we need to give our physical bodies rest, we need to give our minds a rest. I know that my mind can get so busy thinking about so many situations and scenarios.

Prayer Matters

That's when I know my mind needs a rest—a time of cleansing out all of the bad toxic thoughts. Then I can reboot it with life-giving, Spirit-filled thoughts from the word of God.

We also have to take special care of our bodies. I'm in my forties now, and my body is going through so many changes like hormone fluctuations, hot flashes, and even pimples at my age. Gravity has kicked in; where certain body parts used to be, they are now plunging downward. I feel a twinge here and some soreness there. I'm thankful to God for growing older, and one thing that aging has taught me is to take care of my body. I don't take my body for granted anymore. Walking, talking, breathing—all the things I never gave a thought about when I was younger—I now thank God for. Even food that I used to love and enjoy my body rejects now. So I have to be mindful of what I eat. What I put in is what I get out. What we eat is what we become. Consuming fatty foods all the time will make most people obese. There is a small demographic of people who can eat whatever they want and not gain weight, but they might have to deal with clogged arteries, high cholesterol, or other problems that come along with eating high-fat food. If we put good, wholesome food in, we will feel better and are more energized. Most foods that are bad for you tastes so good. But some immediate effects are that you get tired, sleepy, sluggish, gassy, and bloated. Over the long term, you can develop hypertension, high cholesterol, diabetes and many other terrible illnesses—all of which run in my family. Which is why I'm taking steps to do my best with God's help to prevent these conditions. Although these health conditions run in my family, I believe prevention is more than half the battle.

In the past, I haven't always prepared the healthiest food for my family. I've always loved to cook, and some say I'm a pretty good cook. I grew up on Southern "down home food," and that's what I cooked for my family. We didn't eat like this all the time but about sixty per cent of the time. Now, I'm exploring healthier ways to cook the food we love with less fat and sodium. The more I experiment with different flavors and newly found spices and herbs, the more we are starting to like it. The bonus is that we feel so much better. A healthy diet with lots of fruit, vegetables, and good protein has helped me. Incorporating exercise and choosing healthier food options will contribute to overall well-being, good health, and attitude and will help to better ward off running on empty. My problem is that I've always had a hard time exercising and eating right at the same time. With God's help, I know I can do it! The bottom line is that if we fill our bodies with nutritious food and pure water, get regular exercise, and breathe fresh air, then we will have more energy, and our bodies can function at their best.

To function at our best, we must take in spiritual food. Spiritual food is essential, and a spiritual meal should never be missed: "All ate the same spiritual food, and all drank the same spiritual drink. For they drank of that spiritual Rock that followed them, and that Rock was Christ" (1 Cor. 10:3–4). Regular, daily intake of spiritual food is required for spiritual strength. The Word of God is the source of our spiritual food. In it, we find the Source, which strengthens us for life. When we are strong in Christ and in the Word of God, we have the strength to stand in faith when trials come along because we have been nourished with the Word: "If you faint in the day of adversity, your strength is small" (Prov. 24:10). In order to be strong in adversity, feed, meditate, and pray the Word of God. Get full on God's Word. Don't miss a meal, and eat all you want. The more you eat of it, the stronger you will get. Never get empty or depleted. Eat of it every day, multiple times a day if you can. The more you eat of the spiritual food, the more you will desire it, and the stronger you will be.

One other important part of taking care of yourself is having fun. Find a hobby or something recreational that you enjoy doing. After my children became adults, I had to think back on what I enjoyed doing prekids and even premarriage. I'm exploring some new things that I might enjoy doing. I love bike riding when the weather permits. I love being out on the trails in the open fields and having the wind hit my face, feeling the warmth of sun, and smelling the beautiful flowers and trees. When I'm close to nature, I feel close to God. I'm just amazed at God's glorious creations. Having a healthy balance of family, service, work, and recreation is necessary to avoid running on empty. Rest in God and He will refresh you so that you can live your live to the full potential that He created you for. Get your fill of all that God has for you to in order to have a less stressful life. Even if it's hard to find time, designate some time for yourself. It doesn't have to be a spa day, though that sounds great. If you can do it, go for it! But just a few minutes a day to yourself can make a big difference in your energy level, your outlook on life, and your attitude. Do it for yourself. You will not only bless yourself, but others will be blessed with a more rejuvenated you!

Prayer Matter

Father in heaven, I thank You for the awesome privilege of being able to find rest in Your arms. I thank You that I can take Your yoke upon me and find rest for my soul. Lord, I get so tired and weary sometimes. I feel like I carry the weight of the world on my shoulders. So many people depend on me for so many things. It seems that if I don't do "it," it won't get done. I feel like I'm being stretched in so many ways, and there is no more "stretch" left in me.

Lord, give me wisdom to help me to eliminate activities or duties that are not beneficial or are time wasters. Teach me how to prioritize so that I can be more efficient. Help me, Lord, not to be hard on myself when I can't get everything done on my list. I confess that at times I get so busy with the cares of life that I don't spend enough time with You. I know that when I feel this way, it is a call from You to come to You, and You will give me rest. Enable me to relax and rest in You, relinquishing all my strength for Yours.

Take away all my fears, worries, anxieties, and cares. Relieve me from my distress. Endow me with physical, mental, and spiritual Power from on high. I know that there is no limit to the supplies of heaven, for You to give me all that I need to do the work that You called for me to do. Enable me to discern between the things that You have called me to do and the things that You would not have me to do. I want so much to be used by You and for Your glory, but I don't want to wear myself out doing unfruitful things. I know that You will give me the strength that I need for every task.

Father, I ask You to help me to take better care of myself. Give me discipline in the areas of eating healthy and exercise. May I hunger and thirst for more of You and Your Word. Where there is any sickness in my body, I ask You to touch me with Your healing hand and restore me to health. When I lie down at night, I ask that my sleep will be sweet and that when I awake I will be refreshed and energized (Prov. 3:24).

Forgive me when I've allowed bitterness to take root in my life, especially with my family. Help me to not become bitter by self-sacrifice, for I know You gave The Ultimate Sacrifice, Your Son. Forgive me for times that I have been short-tempered, disinterested, disrespectful, or unloving. I know my first ministry is my home with my family. May I always seek peace, and may I put on meekness, goodness, and humility. May my home be a place where peace, love, and joy abide abundantly.

May Your Spirit nourish my mind, soul, and spirit. Refresh me. Lord, I thirst, and I come to You to drink. I believe in You and out of my heart will flow rivers of living water (John 7:3, 38). May I never run on empty; fill me with a never-ending flow of Your Spirit. May I always find intimate time with You to rest in Your arms, be refreshed, and just be. Help me to not grow weary while doing good, for in due season, I will reap if I do not lose heart (Gal. 6:9). I wait on You, Lord, and You shall renew my strength (Isa. 40:31). In Jesus's name, amen.

DON'T BE AFRAID

I sought the Lord, and He heard me, and delivered me from all my fears.

—Psalms 34:4

With everything going on in the world today, it's hard to not be afraid at times. The terrorism, murders, random acts of violence, wars, uncertainties about the future, natural disasters, and health issues are just a few things that cause us to be fearful and worry. Most times, I hate to look at the news because of all the devastating things that are going on in the world. Then there are just the day-to-day concerns that can cause fear, worry, and anxiety, such as worrying about children, getting bills paid on time, mortgages, car notes, or test results from the doctor. It's called life. Jesus says, "In the world we will have tribulation" (John 16:33). Knowing that we are going to have troubles and that we are going to have to face some challenges in this life, how can we not be afraid? I know firsthand of how debilitating fear can be. Fear has stopped me from pursuing some of my dreams. Fear has consumed my mind, and I have experienced thoughts of fear of something terrible happening. I've experienced a fear of flying, fear of doctors, fear of failure, fear of public speaking, fear of doing what God has called me to do, fear of what people think about me, fear of heights, fear of rejection—well, you get the picture.

Fear is a time waster, joy killer, and peace stealer. Fear is a spirit, and God did not give it to us: "For God has not given us a spirit of fear, but of power and love and of a sound mind" (2 Tim. 1:7). If God didn't give it to us, it was sent to destroy us, steal our joy, kill our dreams, and hinder us from being all that God created us to be: "The thief does not come except to steal, and to kill, and to destroy. I have come that they may have life, and that they may have life more abundantly" (John 10:10). Satan wants us to be afraid and paralyzed by fear so that we won't be able live a life that glorifies God and do all that He purposed for us to do. There are countless things to be fearful about in the world today, but that makes for countless things to pray and trust God about. It all comes down to a matter of trust. How much do you trust God to protect and provide for you everything you need?

The Word of God tells us that God did not give us a spirit of fear. If God didn't give it to us, then we know it is from Satan. Fear is debilitating and tormenting, and it was sent by the enemy to keep us from living fruitful and abundant lives and to stop God's plans for us. What has helped me tremendously to get free from fear and other strongholds are prayer and fasting. This means humbling myself before God, abstaining from food for a set amount of time, worshipping Him, and seeking Him with all my heart, mind, and spirit. In my humbling myself to God, I acknowledge Him as Sovereign; I can do nothing on my own, and without Him, I'm nothing. I'll pray, "I need you Lord, more of You, Your will be done in my life as it is in heaven." I am getting into His presence, yielding to Him, surrendering all unto Him, exhausting my will for His will, dying to myself and my fleshly desires, and allowing Him to pour out His love and His precious Holy Spirit upon me. As I humble myself before Him, emptying myself, He fills me and refreshes me with His Spirit. The outpouring of His Spirit fills me and flushes out all impurities in me, the pride, the lusts of the flesh, the fear. Jesus says in the gospel of Mark 9:29, "So He said to them, 'This kind can only come out by nothing but prayer and fasting.'" Jesus is talking about the deaf and dumb spirit in a child. I've personally experience freedom from certain things only by prayer and fasting. I've prayed for years and years against the spirit of fear in my life, and although I've had some deliverance, only through prayer and fasting have I found true deliverance and freedom from the fear that had consumed my life. Are there times when I'm afraid? Yes, but fear does not control my life. I have peace, and when fear tries to consume me, I go to God in prayer and get into His Presence. I keep my eyes on God, not on myself or the circumstance. I don't think about what devastating thing might happen or about the circumstances of what's going on around me. Staying focused on God and what His Word says brings forth light that casts out all darkness, which allows for me to be at rest and in peace. I resist the spirit of fear from the enemy by submitting myself to God and resisting the devil, and the he flees.

(James 4:7).

In times past, I have been deathly afraid of tornadoes. Every time that siren goes off, my mind automatically thinks that a tornado is going to come and rip right through my house. Debris will be flying, walls collapsing, and shattered windows everywhere. It all starts when I'm watching television. I start to read the words at the bottom of the screen, and they say that there is a tornado warning. A tornado warning means that a storm has developed, and it's either produced a tornado or the atmospheric conditions are conducive to producing a tornado. Translated in my mind, I'm thinking, "Here comes the tornado and it's going to hit my house; the roof is going to topple down on top of me and my family in the basement." My heart starts to beat fast as I frantically read on to see what area is supposed to be affected if a tornado might happen to come. While I'm reading the words on the television screen, I start to hear the wailing, distressing sirens go off. I frantically call my daughter to head down to the basement; she finally comes with no sense of urgency at all, almost like I'm overreacting. My husband and I head down, and I start to panic. We look at the news and we see the nearby towns that a tornado was spotted in, and it's slowly heading our way. The newscaster starts naming the towns, and the tornado is getting closer and closer to our residence. My heart starts to beat faster and faster. A combination of the hearing the wail of sirens, watching weather reports, and tracking the tornado has me in a very panicky, fearful state over a tornado that may or may not have happened. As my breathing starts to get labored while I'm pretending like I'm calm, the sirens go silent, the rain eases up, the winds calm, and then the sun comes out. I heave a sigh of relief, and I thank God for watching over us. All that panicking for something that I thought was going to happen. God protected us, but while in the storm, I was not able to trust Him completely. I let myself get all worked up because of fear of something that may or may not have happen. My peace was nowhere to be found, and my joy was out the door. The trust I thought I had was not enough for me to not be fearful. You see, you really don't know how much trust you have in God until you have been put in a situation where you desperately need to trust Him. In that storm, my family and I took shelter and refuge in the basement to protect us, but I didn't trust God enough to be our Shelter to keep us from harm. Instead, I panicked and allowed myself to be fear driven instead of having active faith, knowing that God is our Refuge (Ps. 46:1). Instead of focusing on the weather conditions, a better option would've been for me to focus on God and His promises.

Prayer Matters

In life, it's easy to get caught up in the conditions. If we are not careful, we can start to focus on the negative things that are going on. Or we start to think about things that could or could not happen, and that causes us to get in states of fear, worry, and panic. Sometimes our lives are similar to the tornado warning. The conditions all around us are conducive to a destructive storm coming and doing major damage. When life gets that way, we are either going to be fearful and panic, or we are going to pray in faith and trust God. In those moments of fear, we have the awesome privilege of abiding in the safety of the presence of God, a privilege that I don't take for granted. "He who dwells in the secret place of the Most High Shall abide under the shadow of the Almighty. I will say of the Lord, "He is my refuge and my fortress; My God, in Him I will trust" (Ps. 91:1–2). I thank God for His secret place, His Presence. We are secure and safe in that secret place; all we have to do is seek Him there and draw close to Him. In that secret place there is no fear, and the conditions are conducive for you to be absolutely surrendered to Him and to trust Him completely. In any good relationship you have to have trust. If you don't have trust, you will not have a healthy relationship, and you will always fear that the other person is going to do something bad to damage the relationship. If you don't trust God with your whole heart, you will have those feelings of fear that something bad is going to happen. Trust has to be developed by surrendering yourself to God. By trusting Him in everything you get to know Him, His promises, and His character. You will know that you have nothing to fear for God is with you (Isa. 41:10).

If we keep our eyes set on Him and not set on current or future anticipated adverse conditions, our lives won't be so full of fear: "I have set the Lord always before me; Because He is at my right hand I shall not be moved" (Ps. 16:8). We have to keep our eyes set on Him. Don't get distracted by the storms of life, the winds, and downpours of rain that come in to flood us with fear. We must be like the wise man who built his house on the rock. When the rain descended, the floods came, and the winds blew and beat on that house, it did not fall, because that house was founded on the rock (Matt. 7:24–25). When we set the Lord before us always, continually, we can have peace. This is where we gain victory over fear—in the continual presence of God, and we will not be shaken; we will not be moved. Yes, we will all have moments of fear, and problems in our lives will arise, but we are not to be consumed with fear, paralyzed with fear, and always thinking of the worst. We as believers don't have to be defeated by fear. God will deliver us and go before us. We must seek Him, and in Him we will find freedom and be able to live courageous lives.

Having absolute confidence in God and knowing that God Almighty is with you will help you to live fearlessly. Think about it: God Almighty is with you. God says, "Fear not, for I am with you; Be not dismayed, for I am your God. I will strengthen you, Yes, I will help you, I will uphold you with My righteous right hand" (Isa. 41:10). We don't have to be afraid; He is your God, He loves you, and He will strengthen you. God further reassures us, "For I, the Lord your God, will hold your right hand, saying to you, "Fear not, I will help you" (Isa. 41:13). The Lord your God is always there to hold your hand and to help you through anything. Think of how a child will grab hold of a parent's hand when he or she is afraid. When a mother is taking her child for a walk in the park, and the child hears a dog bark, the child becomes afraid. The mother grabs the hand of the little one and lets him know that she is there to protect him and that there is no need to be afraid; mommy is here. God is saying, "I'm here, fear not, I will help you. The enemy will try to make you afraid. He walks around like a roaring lion, seeking whom he may devour" (1 Pet. 5:8). He may walk around like a roaring lion seeking his prey and try to sneak up on you, but he is already defeated (1 John 3:8). Just grab hold of God's hand, and be aware. Be aware, and pray so that you can discern a trap by

Prayer Matters

the enemy before you walk into it. Walk by faith with God; He will protect you because you are His child, and you have full assurance that you have nothing to be afraid of. God will direct your steps by His word and let no iniquity have dominion over you (Ps. 119:133).

In spite of what we are facing or what we think we are about to face, we must strive to have absolute confidence in God. This confidence comes from seeking God, praying, worshipping, and receiving comfort, protection, love, and revelations of Who He is in His holy presence: "I sought the Lord, and He heard me, and delivered me from all my fears" (Ps. 34:4). We must actively and continually seek and pursue the Lord. In this seeking, we find deliverance from fear. Seeking God involves hanging on to His every Word, meditating on His Word, and allowing it to saturate our spirits. Abide in His presence and let Him overtake you with His love and comfort. Let there be no motive except for Him to reveal Himself to you. He will reveal His heart, His attributes, and His will to you. He will reveal Himself as your Protector, Provider, Deliverer, and Refuge. You become one with Him, and you rest from your fears and worries. He pours out His perfect love upon you, and fear cannot abide there: "There is no fear in love; but perfect love casts out fear, because fear involves torment. But he who fears has not been made perfect in love" (1 John 4:18).

God loves you perfectly and entirely. In knowing that He loves you, you know that He cares about, will provide for, and will protect you. We must have a true revelation of our Father. Trusting Him in complete surrender of every area of our lives will allow for us to live lives of progressive faith. We must be fully convinced that God's Word is true and that He will do what He says. We must trust Him entirely for everything we need and in every situation, no matter how bad it seems to be. Ask yourself, "What does God say in His word about my situation?" Believe Him and trust Him. If we truly place this absolute trust in Him, then there is no need to fear. If we seek Him with our whole hearts, then He will hear and

165

will deliver us from our fears. Pursue Him like never before. Learn from Him; great is the peace of His children for they are taught of the Lord (Isa. 54:13). Because of the Lord's great love and care for us, we don't have to be consumed with fear. Keep focused on Him and don't allow fear to distract you and keep you from where God wants you to go and being all that He created you to be: "I have set the Lord always before me; because He is at my right hand I shall not be moved" (Ps. 16:8). When we fix our eyes on God, we won't get blindsided by fear. See, He is at our right hand. He is on our side to protect us from being blindsided by fear, and we will be able to stand. He covers us, and under His wings we can take refuge (Ps. 91:4). He also goes before us (Deut. 31:8). Let's see, He is at our right hand, on our sides, covers us, and goes before us. That pretty much covers everything. If you think about it that way, what do we have to be afraid about? Praise God! With God, we can stand in courage, confidence, and faith. Set your eyes before Him forevermore. No need to be afraid, He's got you.

Prayer Matter

Father, I come to You in the name of Jesus, thanking You for being at my right hand, on my side, covering me, and going before me. Therefore, I don't have to be bound by fear. Because of Your love, I will fear no evil, for You are with me, Lord, and Your Word and Your Spirit comfort me. In the midnight hour when my mind tends to worry and fear torments me, I know I can seek comfort in You and call on the name of Jesus. You will calm my fears and bring me to a place of rest.

I confess that at times I have let fear control my life. Forgive me, Lord. A life lived in fear is torture, and I ask You, Lord, to free me from the spirit of fear. As I come into Your Presence, I ask that You will give me faith instead of fear, and give me peace instead of worry. When I'm timid, help me to be bold. Replace anxiety with calmness and with a spirit of rest. Give me Your power in place of my panic. When my mind is not at rest, make my mind sound. Help me to meditate on Your Word, so the peace of You will guard my mind.

Prayer Matters

Lord, there's so much going on in the world today, if I'm not careful, I could easily live a life of fear and panic. Help me to know wisdom and be watchful and prayerful. I thank You for the precious blood of Jesus to protect, deliver, and set me free. Lord, protect me and my family and keep us safe from hurt, harm, or danger. Wherever our feet step today, I apply the blood of Jesus. May we freely receive Your perfect love that casts out all fear so that we can be free to be all that you predestined us to be.

Father, enable me to resist the enemy when he tries to torment my mind. For I know if I submit to You and resist him, he will flee in Jesus's name (James 4:7). When my eyes start to wander and I get distracted by life's problems, redirect my eyes to You. In You is where my peace lies. If I keep my mind set on You, You will keep me in perfect peace because I trust You (Isa. 26:3). I know that if I really trust You, I will not be afraid.

I ask You to mold me into a woman of courage and a bold witness for You! Give me enthusiasm and optimism to fulfill all Your plans for me. I surrender all of my life to You, Lord, trusting You with every part. In You I have victory over fear. I know You are with me, beside me, for me, and the very life of You is living in me, strong and courageous: "You are my light and my salvation. Whom shall I fear? I will walk by faith not by fear. You are the strength of my life. Of whom shall I be afraid?" (Ps. 27:1). May I live a life of adamant faith and relentless courage that is pleasing to You, in Your Spirit of power, love, and a sound mind. In Jesus's name I pray, amen (2 Tim. 1:7).

167

RIGHT RELATIONSHIPS

Do not be deceived: "Evil company corrupts good habits."

—1 Corinthians 15:33

Have you ever been in a bad relationship and wondered, "How did I get into this mess and how do I get out of it?" I have been in this situation before. I'm sure that most of us have, whether it be romantic relationships or maybe betrayal at the hands of those whom we thought were our friends. In some cases, bad relationships can involve family members, and there can be conflict and unresolved issues.

The quality of life that we live is in part determined by the relationships that we have. The people who we most surround around ourselves with have a major impact on our emotions, values, ideas, decisions, and goals. I've seen my own life get derailed by associating myself with the wrong people. I've also seen many people's lives cut short by associating with the wrong crowd. Relationships are a part of life and are much needed in life. If not for relationships, the world would be a lonely place. It's only human to desire companionship and friendship, someone who has similar interests, someone to talk to, and someone around whom you can just be yourself and kick back. Where the problem comes in is when at times, some relationships are not healthy for us to be in. Some relationships are easy to determine as toxic but they are hard to get out of. In fact, we might have known from the beginning that it wasn't a good idea to even pursue these relationships. All the "red flags" were waving, but we followed our hearts.

Then there are strained family relationships. Trying to resolve issues and reconcile with some family can be difficult because of deep hurt, betrayal, and bitterness. A marriage relationship that is ending in divorce is a very delicate and traumatic situation. The hurt is overwhelming and your heart is crushed into microscopic pieces. The hurt, anger, and betrayal leaves you in a haze, numb, but you keep it moving for the kids' sakes. You worry about how you are going to make ends meet. You reflect back on what you might've done wrong to cause this to happen. Am I not pretty enough? Did I not give him enough attention? All those years of giving with all your heart seemed to be wasted and unappreciated. Consider a breakup: You had hopes of this man being your husband, but he betrayed you. Your heart hurts so bad that it aches, and to make things worse, you still love him and long to be with him. It's like you can't live with him, and you feel like your life cannot go on without him.

There are all kinds of relationships in our lives. Our relationships with our spouses, children, parents, and siblings are often our closest bonds. However, some may have friends closer than their blood relatives. Then there are relationships that just drain the life right out of you. You know those friends—when you see their names pop up on your phone and you don't want to answer. It's always all about them, and when you talk to them you can never seem to get a word in about what's going on in your life, not that they even care anyway. Some relationships are just not healthy; they are draining, one-sided, negative, or bad influences. Then there are the life-giving relationships. These friends bring a smile to your face, and they are faithful. You both are always there for each other. You're glad when the phone lights up with that friend's name. It's not a one-sided relationship—it goes both ways, and he or she has interest in how you are doing and what's going on in your life. You both listen to and encourage the other. You hope and pray the best for each other; there is no judgment, and you can be transparent. He or she loves, cares for, and respects you.

Deciding what are healthy relationships, unhealthy relationships, relationships that need to broken off, and relationships that are worth working toward reconciliation is important. All these decisions are based on our most important relationship: our relationship with God. God gives us tons of relationship information in His Word. In any relationship, there is an exchange that takes place. This can be either positive or negative, and in most cases, it's both. If there are too many negative exchanges, this may be a sign that you need to subtract that person from your life. Relationships have to be reciprocated. If one person is always giving and the other is always taking, then that's not a relationship—that is someone taking advantage of another person. If one person is always available for the other and it's not reciprocated, I would question if that relationship was genuine. However, I have very good friends who I don't talk to very often, but in our hearts we have a bond, and we have genuine love for another. If we need one another, we are there, no questions asked.

Association is so important. If you want to see the kind of person you are or who you will become, look at who you are hanging around: "Do not be deceived: 'Evil company corrupts good habits'" (1 Cor. 5:33). Paul says, "Do not be deceived"—this is letting me know that the possibility is great for people to be ensnared into ungodly living if they associate themselves with ungodly people

Prayer Matters

regularly. That's why the word of God tells us to, "Come out from among them and be separate, says the Lord" (2 Cor. 6:17). We have to live in this world, and we are called to witness and spread the message of the gospel to the unsaved, but we are to maintain integrity in the world with no compromise. We have to live and function in this world, but we also are to show the love of Christ to everyone without compromising our commitment to God.

Jesus is our example. Jesus associates with sinners but only to bring them into repentance and salvation. "Now after John was put in prison, Jesus came to Galilee, preaching the gospel of the kingdom of God, and saying, 'The time is fulfilled, and the kingdom of God is at hand. Repent, and believe in the gospel.'" (John 1:14-15) Jesus preaches the gospel of the kingdom of God, repentance, and calls them to believe in the gospel. Jesus's life demonstrates perfectly of how we are to strive to be.

We should not associate closely with nonbelievers who reject the gospel message. There have been a couple of people who I've really liked and have enjoyed their friendship, but we don't have a lot in common anymore—mainly Jesus. Once I started living for Jesus, some of the old friendships changed, and some gradually came to an end. See, when God starts to transform your life, your desires start to change. Some of the things you were once interested in, you are no longer interested in anymore. What you used to do, God delivered you from. Moreover, if you start sharing the gospel of Jesus Christ with these friends, they might distance themselves from you with no effort on your part. When you present the word of God to people, they are either going to be drawn to Christ, or they will be driven away from the Christ in you. That means that some people will not want to associate themselves with you. You might not get the phone calls, the visits, or the invites. Don't take it personal; it's Christ in you that they are rejecting. The light of Christ exposes their darkness, and they don't feel comfortable around you anymore, or they don't feel comfortable doing certain things around you either out of respect for you or conviction from God. Some just reject truth altogether, and they don't want to hear it, or they're just not ready to receive it and make changes. It doesn't necessarily mean that they don't love you. It just means that they don't have anything in common with you anymore. Is it hurtful? Yes, at times, but the more you seek the Lord and get to really know Him, He fills the void in your heart, and He not only fills the void, but He fills the void to overflow. He is The Friend who will stick to you closer than a brother (Prov. 18:24). He won't let you down. He's always there for you. You can talk to Him anytime, anywhere. He takes you as you are, and He loves you, no matter what: "Delight yourself also in the Lord, and He will give you the desires of your heart" (Ps. 37:4). He will give you the desires of your heart according to His will. He knows that you desire friendship, and He will bless you with like-minded friends, friends who love the Lord, friends who will pray with you and encourage you, and friends with whom you can have a good time.

Family relationships can be more delicate. Family in most cases include the people who know you the most, and they are the closest to your heart. God initiated the family in the beginning with Adam and Eve; He blesses them and says to them, "Be fruitful and multiply" (Gen. 1:28). Their son Cain kills his brother Abel (Gen. 4:8). Why? Because of jealousy, pride, and anger. God doesn't respect Cain's offering, but God does respect Abel's offering (Gen. 4:3). Cain's jealousy and anger provokes him to kill his brother. Sibling jealousy and rivalry is nothing new, it has been around since the beginning of time. Another example is Jacob and Esau. Jacob and Esau's battle starts very early on in their mother's womb (Gen. 25:22). No need to wait until birth to get the rivalry started. When Rebekah gives birth to the twins, Esau comes out first and Jacob afterward, his hand holding Esau's heel (Gen. 25:24–26). This struggle between siblings continues. Esau goes on to sell his birthright to his brother Jacob for stew. Isaac, their father, favors

Esau, while Rebekah favors Jacob. Some parents today have their "favorite" child. Rebekah orchestrates and devises events so that Isaac could bless Jacob, and Jacob goes along with it. Esau hates his brother Jacob because of the blessing from his father. Later on in life, the brothers reconcile, and Jacob even blesses his brother Esau (Gen. 33:4–11).

When someone in your family who is supposed to love you and protect you hurts you either emotionally or physically, it devastates you, and even though years may have gone by, you may still have scars, pain, bitterness, anger, resentment, and sometimes hate. In addition, the hurt or betrayal affects your future relationships. You may have trust issues, abandonment issues, or you may not be emotionally available. Those "walls" are up, doors shut, and it's going to take God's power to break those walls down and open the doors for you to be able to trust and love the way God created you to.

Unresolved issues, not choosing to forgive, confusion, jealousies, envy, offense, miscommunication, and favoritism are some things that cause dissension and division in families. Breakdown of the family either through divorce, holding grudges, betrayal, abuse, or abandonment is tough. Often other members of the family feel as if they have to take sides, and this can cause further division. Reconciliation is possible if the family members who are involved are ready to heal, move forward, leave the past in the past, and forgive. It is a two-way street. If the other person is not willing to meet you halfway, then that is their choice, and it's their problem—not yours. You can only be accountable for you. Do all that you know is right to do, and leave the rest up to God. Unfortunately, in some families, horrible things happen such as molestation, incest, and physical abuse. These things are often kept secret while people are obviously suffering from the devastating abuse they suffered. Some can't maintain a healthy relationship, while some use drugs or alcohol to numb the pain.

To forgive or not to forgive? A person may choose to forgive an abuser, but having a relationship with that person may not be an option for them. It can be painful and problematic at family functions when the person who has hurt you and severely altered your life is there. Some people are able to forgive, some not.

The most important thing that you can do for yourself in this situation is to forgive. (Matthew 6:14-15) As hard as it may be, we have to, and God will give us the grace to do it. Forgiveness is a process of believing in God to help you to do what you cannot do on your own: forgive. Forgiveness does not mean a free pass back into your life. It means you forgive someone for what he or she has done to you, and now you can move forward and not be held a prisoner by the actions perpetrated by someone else against you.

A former classmate of mine had a very troubled relationship with her mother, to say the least. As a child she was given to her father to raise because her mom was doing her own thing. Her mother had become addicted to drugs and began to live a very reckless life. As a teenager the young lady became very promiscuous and rebellious. During this time resentment and bitterness started to build up towards her estranged mother. She saw her mother on occasion but they never developed a normal mother-daughter relationship. As a result, the young lady suffered from abandonment issues and feelings of rejection. Although her father and other family members assured her of their love for her, and showed her in so many ways, no one could take the place of her mother and fill the void of her mother's love. No one's love seemed to reach the depths of her shattered heart.

The young lady's heart was hardened. She seemed to reject genuine love from her family but would open her heart to counterfeit love from abusive men and people who meant her no good. The only love she really longed for was from her mother, all else was just a substitute. In order to fill that void in her life she got

Prayer Matters

involved in numerous of abusive relationships and she eventually got involved with drugs. She was gradually turning into the person that she longed for and resented the most. The person who she was determined not to be like; her mother.

Later on in her life she and her mother would try to reconcile but to this day they haven't been able to patch things up. The mother is very remorseful. She admits that she's made a lot of mistakes. She has now gotten her life on track. Glory to God! All she wants now is for her daughter to forgive her and she wants a chance to be in her daughter's life. Her daughter can't seem to forgive her mom. She has so much built up anger and frustration.

The love that the daughter longed for, searched for, yearned for, is now available to her but she rejects it. She wants her mother to feel the pain that abandonment and rejection brings. Deep down her heart is longing for affection, love and acceptance. She yearns for her mother's embrace. She's dreamt of being in the arms of her mother and her mother telling her that she loves her. But the door of bitterness and resentment is closed and she refuses to let her mother in. She can't find it in her heart to forgive. She can't move forward, and neither can her mom. They both are stuck in a painful cycle that can't seem to be stopped.

To make matters worse, that same young lady that was abandoned by her mom, she has now abandoned her young daughter. The wheel of rejection and despair in this family keeps going around and around. I often wonder if forgiveness could be a start to reconciliation and healing for both the mom and the daughter. I don't know, but holding on to bitterness always seems to hurt the person whose holding onto it more. Once you let it go, it can't hurt you anymore.

Everyone wants and needs companionship. I've heard some women say, "I don't need a man." I beg to differ. I believe everyone deep down wants to love and wants to be loved. The relationship between a man and a woman is something that God ordained. God says, "It is not good that man should be alone; I will make him a helper comparable to him" (Gen. 2:18). It's not good for man to be alone, so God makes a woman (Gen. 2:22). My daughters are of the marrying age now. My oldest is recently married and my youngest is a "lady in waiting." When my daughters were teenagers, they had lists of all the attributes that they wanted in their husbands. These lists included what they wanted their husbands to look like, including certain heights, perfect white teeth, and specific builds. Other characteristics included being caring, funny, having a stable career, and the list went on and on, but the most important attribute was that the man would know the Lord. Yes, their lists were long, maybe a little superficial, and a little unrealistic, but their desire was for godly men. Their lists were very different as far as what they wanted in their potential husbands, but they both had God in common. I was very happy about that because whom they decide to spend their lives with is very important, and the idea of them getting involved with someone whom God had not intended for them troubles me to even think about. My hope was that they would not stray too far from that list, especially from the godly character traits. If a man has the godly character traits, everything else will be covered. When he loves the Lord and follows Him, he will be a great leader for his family. He will be loving, respectful, a good provider, wise, strong, and humble: "The steps of a good man are ordered by the Lord" (Ps. 27:23a).

Waiting on God, having discernment, and being prayerful is necessary so that you will not be deceived. Believe me, you do not want the man whom God has not ordained to be your husband. Settling, compromising, and not being patient will cause you a lot of heartache and trouble in the long run: "Do not be unequally yoked together with unbelievers. For what fellowship has righteousness with lawlessness?" (2 Cor. 6:14). When a believer

Prayer Matters

is yoked together with a nonbeliever, it makes for a struggle. This isn't to say it won't work because I know marriages where it has worked. It just makes it more difficult, and it can be more of a struggle. One will want to go one way, and the other person will want to go another. It's a battle, with each partner going in a different direction, while really you are going nowhere. Someone has to compromise. It's either going to be you or the other person. Sadly, some, including myself, have compromised in relationships. Compromising shows that you really don't trust the Lord as much as you think. Each time you compromise, you are giving up more and more of what you know is right. More and more of yourself and all that you know to be true is compromised. Each time you compromise, you lower your standards little by little. It's like the list of attributes that my daughters had—only the list gets smaller and smaller. You think to yourself, "That quality is not that important, I'll scratch that one off." Then one leads to two, and as time goes by, you scratch off a couple more. Before you know it, the only qualities on the list are a job and nice teeth. I'm being funny here, but many women's "lists" are getting shorter and shorter because they are tired of waiting.

The main reason why there's so much compromise in relationships is because many are not patient in waiting. I know, some have been waiting for a long time, but it's better to wait on God's best than to settle for less. If settling for less means pain, heartache, infidelity, and no trust or respect, then I'll wait for God to bless me; it will be worth the wait. It's like choosing a small pebble (settling for the man whom you know is not God's best for you) when all you have to do is wait, and you can get the diamond (the man of God). Some settle for the pebble just to have something. Something is better than nothing, right? Not! Wait for the big rock, the big diamond, the man that God has for you! God is able to do exceedingly, abundantly above all that you ask or think, according to the power that works in you (Eph. 3:20). No matter what age you are, if you are single, I encourage you to delight yourself in the Lord, wait on Him, and trust Him. God blesses faithfulness and obedience.

The Bible says in Amos 3:3, "Can two walk together, unless they agree?" In order to walk together, you have to agree on the direction you are going in. If people are going in two different directions, you will never meet and come together. In fact, you will end up going further and further apart. In a marriage especially, you need agreement. First, you must be in agreement with the Word of God. God has to be the center of the marriage. I've been married a long time, and let me tell you, without God it would not have lasted. So many times, we could've given up. Only by God's abundant grace and mercy did my husband and I tough it out and commit to making it work. It's not easy, but it's worth it. I married my best friend and we are closer today than ever before. He encourages me in the Lord. He prays for me and with me. When I'm emotional, he's my voice of reason. When I'm feeling down, he makes me laugh. He makes me smile when I want so badly to stay mad at him.

Even though my husband and I have been married for a long time, it does not mean that we still don't have to put in the work to have a healthy relationship. In some ways you have to work at it more because you get comfortable and you start to take each other for granted. You've been together for so long, you finish each other's sentences, so the conversations can get boring. You do the same things over and over again. You can almost tell what the other is thinking and feeling without saying a word. Things can get pretty predictable if you don't keep it spicy. It is imperative that you make time for each other. Nurture the marriage. Communicate. I know we've all heard this one a thousand times, but it is crucial to communicate if you want your marriage to work. Communication is a two-sided conversation of talking and listening.

May I point out that tuning out is not part of communication. I had become a pro at tuning my husband out, particularly when I didn't want to hear what he had to say, wasn't interested in what he had to say, or may have heard the same story before at least three times. Either way, I was wrong. Being disinterested or showing disinterest in the things that your spouse is talking about or things that are important to him is not conducive to a healthy marriage. This goes both ways of course. Yes, there have been plenty of times when I'm trying to tell my husband something and he hasn't heard a word that has come out of my mouth. As frustrating as it is, my timing can be off at times. Obviously, if he's watching sports, then that is not a good time to strike up a conversation about something that can wait. Sometimes I'll be watching a really good movie and my husband wants to narrate it, talking through the movie, attempting to predict what is going to happen. So I just press the pause button on the remote until he finishes talking or he realizes that I'm agitated and stops. Small things—but small things add up and can be rather annoying and can cause disinterest because it's "getting on your nerves." It's also very important to have your own hobbies and interests. Just because you're married does not mean that you have to spend all of your time together. A man needs his time and so does a woman. This helps so that the time spent together is never stale; it makes it quite lively.

The Bible says in Romans 12:10, "Be kindly affectionate to one another with brotherly love, in honor giving preference to another." I love the first part of this scripture: be kindly affectionate to one another. Showing love and affection is very important in a relationship, especially in a marriage. It's one thing to say that you love a person, but love has to be shown. Greet each other with a kiss. Cuddle sometimes, without a motive, if you know what I mean. It does not always have to lead up to sexual intimacy. In some marriages, the only time affection is shown is when one person wants to have sex. This makes the intimacy seem more like a duty instead of two people making love to each other. Subsequently, when love is shown frequently outside the bedroom by gentle touches, washing dishes, doing the laundry, giving flowers, or even unexpected texts of appreciation during the day, it keeps the marriage from being predictable, and it helps to keep the marriage intriguing.

The second part of the scripture urges us to prefer the other before ourselves. When you get past "I" all the time and seek the best for your mate, it is a self-sacrificial love. I'm not saying to not think of yourself, but always consider your mate and honor him. When married, two become one (Mark 10:8). Whatever affects one also affects the other for good or bad. When both spouses seek the happiness and well-being of the other, it makes for a good, stable marriage. It takes a lot of compromise, but if you put in the work, like a good job, it pays well.

When both people are submitted to the authority of Christ and make Him the center of their marriage, the marriage is strong. When God is invited into the marriage, things go better. Problems will arise because nobody is perfect, but when God is placed at the centermost of the marriage union, it will stand through all the tests: "Though one may be overpowered by another, two can withstand him. And a threefold cord is not quickly broken" (Eccles. 4:12). I cannot stress the importance of praying together with your spouse. This is an area that some couples struggle with. There is power when a husband and wife can stand in agreement in prayer. Amazing things happen when a husband and wife pray together. It draws both of them closer together by drawing close to God in prayer. It is so special and intimate, knowing God is present in that moment in union with you and your mate. Make prayer time with your spouse a priority, even if it's once a week or whenever you both can find a mutual convenient time to pray. Make an appointment with God and you will be blessed and amazed. When Christ is the Cord holding you and your spouse together, nothing can tear you apart. He will pull you closer and closer to each other, and the more each of you grow in Christ, the more you will grow more in love with each other.

Prayer Matters

Good relationships are very important parts of life. Some we choose and some we are born into. Being prayerful and allowing God to lead you in all relationships are the keys. When we get into relationships that we know that are not healthy for us, and we know that it is not God's will for us to be in these toxic relationships, God will give you the strength to be able to let go. Only in looking to Him will you find the strength to do so. Knowing the difference of when to let go and when to hold on to a relationship has to be prayed about and lined up with the Word of God. Some people aren't meant to go with you all the way. When traveling on a train, people get off at different stops, such as our life's journey. Toxic people poison your life, no matter who they are. Toxic people bring drama, negativity, guilt, discouragement, and criticism to your life. Slowly, they poison your life and take your enthusiasm, your joy, and your peace. Whomever is eliminated from your life either by you, them, or God, He will replace with so much better (Read Matt. 12:50). Once you let go, you make room for the person He has for you. In the meantime, be patient, continue to give your whole heart to Him, and seek His will for your life. As you seek first God's kingdom, He will add to your life people who love you, respect you, care for you, pray for you and with you, and encourage you in Him. Friends and maybe some family have betrayed or disowned you, but God never will. We are adopted into His beautiful family and He is our Father (Rom. 8:15). He never leaves us, never disowns us and His love is unconditional and forever.

Prayer Matter

I thank You, Everlasting Father, for choosing me to be a part of Your wonderful family. I thank You for loving me completely and fully. I am accepted in the Beloved (Eph. 1:6). Where others have been unfaithful, You have remained more than faithful. Where others have left me, You have never left me alone. Where people have disappointed me, my hope in You has never been disappointed.

Father, I ask You to reveal to me any relationships that you have not ordained in my life. Lord, when you reveal them to me, I ask You to give me the strength to let them go. Where I have compromised relationships, already knowing that they were not Your will for me, I ask for Your forgiveness. I ask You to forgive me for allowing my own fleshly desires to take precedence over Your will for my life. Help me walk in Your Spirit, Lord. I know as I delight myself in You, You will give me the desires of my heart according to Your will.

Lord, help me to forgive the people in my life who have hurt me, abandoned me, or rejected me. Touch and heal my broken heart. Take away the sting of the hurt that they have caused me so that I can move on with my life. I pray, Lord, that they know You as their personal Lord and Savior and that they will give their lives to You.

Lord, where You see a need to heal broken relationships, I ask you to bring restoration and reconciliation. Where You see fit to bring closure to a relationship, I ask for Your will to be done and for You to give me strength to have closure and accept Your will. Enable me to move forward, trusting you with all my heart.

Free me from all disappointments and letdowns from people. My hope is in You. My relationship with You is the most important relationship I will ever have. I will always seek You first, and know all other things shall be added unto me (Matt. 6:33).

Lord, give me wisdom and discernment so that I will choose right relationships that bring You glory. I don't want to disappoint You. Where I have been impatient in waiting, Lord, give me patience to wait for Your best for me. May my time of waiting be spent with You and doing the things that You would have for me to do for You. Help me not to be deceived, and give me strength by Your Spirit not to settle for the "pebble."

Father, I ask You to bring into my life like-minded people whose goal is to live for You, people who have godly characters, and people with the mind of God and hearts like Yours. I know that there are no perfect people, Lord,

Prayer Matters

I just ask for people in my life who are striving for the upward call in Christ Jesus with all humility in service to You. I'm seeking people who want to help others up and not tear others down, people whose foremost relationship is with You in whom all other relationships are based. In Jesus's name I pray, amen.

A LIFE HIDDEN WITH CHRIST

Set your mind on things above, not on things on the earth. For you died, and your life is hidden with Christ in God.

—1 Colossians 3:2–3

When I was a kid, I used to love to play hide-and-go-seek. I remember the anticipation of waiting for my childhood friends to count to ten as I frantically looked for places to hide. I needed places where my friends could never find me, somewhere inconspicuous. I had to be extra quiet when my secret spots were found, trying hard not to laugh or breathe too hard, or I would be found out. After so many games, it got more difficult to find places to hide. If you were the seeker, you had to look around high and low, behind the oak tree, on the other side of the house, up in the tree, behind a bush, or in a box. The seeker had to cover his eyes so that he couldn't see where everyone was going. After counting, the seeker would shout, "Ready or not, here I come!" This game was so simple, yet so much fun and interactive. Many long, hot summer days were spent playing hide-and-go-seek.

In playing the game I didn't know exactly where I was going to hide each time; I just figured it out as I went along. Sometimes it turned out good and other times, not so good. Sometimes when I thought I was hiding, I was so plainly seen, just as with our walk with God. Sometimes we may think that our lives are hidden with Christ, but there are parts of our lives that are exposed and not completely hidden, and if some parts are exposed, then you are exposed. Just like in the game of hide-and-go-seek, if you are hiding and the seeker only sees your foot, you are revealed and unconcealed. Life is definitely not a game, and not nearly as simple and full of fun. Although just as in the game of hide and go seek, in our lives here on earth we are to hide, but hide with Christ: "You are my hiding place and my shield" (Ps. 119:114ᵃ). We are to go: "Go therefore and make disciples of all nations, baptizing them in the name of the Father and of the Son and of the Holy Spirit" (Matt. 28:19). We are to seek the Lord: "Seek the Lord and His strength; Seek His face forever more" (1 Chron. 16:11).

The Bible tells us, "If then you were raised with Christ, seek those things which are above, where Christ is, sitting at the right hand of God" (Col. 3:1). Our spiritual lives are hidden with Christ so we must look to Him. The things above are eternal; things in this life are temporary, lose value, and fade away.

Do not lay up for yourselves treasures on earth, where moth and rust destroy and where thieves break in and steal, but lay up for yourselves treasures in heaven, where neither moth nor rust destroys, and where thieves do not break in and steal. For where you treasure is, there your heart will be also. (Matt. 6:19–21)

To function in this world, there are things we have to do. We have to work, pay bills, eat, and take care of ourselves and others. This scripture does not mean to not have a savings or to not plan for retirement or our children's college educations. It just means that our treasures, our most valuable, priceless things, are to be sought after from above and laid up in heaven. Sometimes we can worry so much about this world that we neglect or forget the things above, which are the most important things. This world and its desires are passing away (1 John 2:17). It's OK to invest in, plan, and enjoy life, but our priority should always be to seek things above where Christ is. The spiritual blessings in heavenly places are most important and eternal (Eph. 1:3). In fact, setting our eyes on things above helps us to better cope with the trials that we encounter here on earth.

The Bible tells you to "set your mind on things above, not on things on the earth" (Col. 3:2). There are so many things that can distract us and cause us to take our minds off God, and before you know it, your mind is so full of clutter and worry that you become overwhelmed. That is why it is imperative that your life be hidden with Christ. When your life is hidden and concealed with Christ in God, the cares of this world will not overtake you or overwhelm you. You will have a more eternal perspective, and you will be assured that with Christ and Christ in you, you are protected to survive hectic and difficult times.

"For you died, and now your life is hidden with Christ in God" (Col. 3:3). We must die to sin and put off our old mortal natures. The more we walk in obedience to God, the more we are hidden with Him. As we walk in the Spirit and turn away from the world and its desires, the more we are alive in Christ. This putting off the "old man" is sanctification, and it is a process. The old life I used to live is now dead; it is no more. Now I have a new life that is in Christ. Have I messed up? Plenty of times, and I've wanted to give up plenty of times.

Prayer Matters

I've had feelings that I just couldn't live up to the standard of godly living. My mind-set was all wrong. I thought my salvation was based on works, so every time I didn't do something right, I got frustrated, discouraged, and wanted to give up. See, I didn't understand the grace of God. God's grace is sufficient because of what Jesus did on the cross. He died for every sin that I would ever commit. He already knew that I would make mistakes and fall short. His love is just that great for us—that He took all the cruel punishment, ridicule, pain, and humiliation for us anyway. He died, was buried, and rose so that we could have everlasting lives and so we could have the awesome opportunity to have lives hidden with Him. Just as Jesus died on the cross, so too are we to die to ourselves and our sinful natures. Our old lives must be buried and we are to walk in the newness of life (Rom. 6:4).

To be hidden with Christ is to unite our will with the will of God. When we abide in Christ, we are one with Him. In Christ, you are who you were created to be in His image. His attributes become yours, His desires for your life become your desires as you delight yourself in Him. The more we seek His will and commit to doing it, the more we discover His unconditional love for us, His great faithfulness, and His mercy that lasts forever. He provides a love that heals every wound, comforts every hurt, supplies all your needs, and gives you peace like a never-ending river. It's an indescribable love, a knowing in your heart that He loves and cares for you and that He is always there. This love compels us to please Him.

For the love of Christ compels us we, because we judge thus: that if One died for all, then all died; and He died for all, that those who live should live no longer for themselves, but for Him who died for them and rose again. Therefore, from now on, we regard no one according to the flesh. Even though we have known Christ according to the flesh, yet now we know Him thus no longer. Therefore, if anyone is in Christ, he is a new creation, old things have passed away; behold all things have become new. (2 Cor. 5:14–18)

Once we are in Christ, we no longer live for ourselves. Our foremost priority and ambition should be to please The Father (2 Cor. 5:9). Whether in public or in private, seek to please the Lord in all you do, and if you happen to mess up, don't give up. God gives us new mercy every day. He's just that good!

I have always been a "people pleaser," and I have always been overly concerned about what people thought about me. People's approval meant too much to me. I'm just getting to a place in my life that as long as I am pleasing the Lord, I don't concern myself about what other people think of me. Am I all the way there yet? No, but I'm well on my way. If God is pleased and accepts me, then that has to be enough. I know that I can't please everybody, and like my mom told me when I was a little girl, "Everybody is not going to like you." The truth is that if everybody liked me now, I would truly have to examine myself. If I was adored by the world, then something in me must be worldly. My goal is to be holy, for God is holy (1 Pet. 1:16). A life hidden with Christ in God is a life hidden from the people who knew you when you used to "turn up," as the young people say now. They don't recognize the new you. Your life is so hidden that they don't see the "old" you. Your life is renewed, and some can't identify with you anymore. In fact, they may think that you have lost your mind or are too radical. Some may withdraw from you, and glory to God, some will be drawn to God by His Spirit in you.

When we hide with Christ, we have everything we need. Believe in Him with all your heart and mind, and then receive all from Him, in Him. Our lives must be totally surrendered to the Lordship of Jesus. No part of our lives will remain uncovered when we submit every part of it to Him. Many times I thought an area of my life was surrendered to God, but it wasn't. It's like having a bruise or scratch on your body that you didn't know was there. You were not looking for it, but when you showered, you just happened to notice it. In fact, you didn't even feel it, and you wondered how it got there in the first place. There are areas of our lives where we may have had blemishes that we didn't even know were there until God brought them to our attention. You wonder, "How did that get there? Where did this bitterness come from? Why am I so easily offended? Why do I care so much about what people think of me? Why do I always have to be right? Why do I have a tendency to be envious of people?"

When God brings these things to your attention, you have to examine yourself, and He will reveal to you how it got there. There is always a cause and an effect. For example, I've always overcompensated when it comes to my children. One area that I did this is in was chores. I often did everything from cleaning their rooms, vacuuming and washing dishes every night. My children really were not required to do a lot of chores. I realized that I did this because growing up I had to do it all. While my mom worked, I had to cook, clean, do laundry, and other household duties. I always felt that I missed out on some of my childhood. In my mind, I wanted my children to enjoy being a kid and do kid things. So I was lenient in this area with them. If I had known what I know now, they would have been given more responsibilities. Another example is that in the past, I never felt good enough. God revealed to me that it came from when my parents divorced and my father started a new family. Those are just a couple of my blemishes that have been cleansed, washed, and healed by God. God will apply His healing balm to our blemishes and they will fade away if we allow Him to. We can't attempt to heal them on our own, covering up with quick fixes and substitutes with no real healing. Covering up does not bring healing. Expose it, and ask God to heal you from the inside out. Only He can heal us completely, made whole and new in Him.

As we walk in the Spirit, our "blemishes" start to disappear, and the light that is in Christ shines through us more and more (Eph. 5:8). When we are in Christ, He fills us with His Spirit. I've found that it's good to seek to be filled with the Spirit of the Living God, but it is better to seek the Filler, seek the Living God. As you seek Him, you will be filled with all of His fullness, and your life will be found in Him and lived for Him, wholeheartedly dependent and yielded to God. Your life is no longer your own; in your complete surrender, your heart will whisper, "Lord, not my will, but your will be done through me, for your glory." You will display the heart of the Father, in turn getting your eyes off of yourself and onto the purpose for which you were created. You now have unity with Christ, and what is on His heart is placed in your heart to do the work of the Father: "So Jesus said to them again, 'Peace to you! As the Father has sent Me, I also send you.' And when He had breathed on them, and said to them, 'Receive the Holy Spirit'" (John 20:21–22). The Holy Spirit released through you empowers you to do great things for God's kingdom. A life hidden with Christ is ripe and ready to produce fruit for God's kingdom.

The life hidden with Christ produces the fruit of the Spirit. Galatians 5:22–23 says, "But the fruit of the Spirit is love, joy, peace, longsuffering, kindness, goodness, faithfulness, gentleness, self-control." These fruits are for us to live lives that bring glory to God, but they enable us to better serve others. A life truly hidden with Christ will exhibit these attributes to people. Jesus did not give His life for Himself; He gave it for us. Because of His unconditional love for us, He gave His life. We are to be His example. Our lives should show forth the same love for others as Jesus's did for us. We can only show this love by abiding in Jesus wholeheartedly. It's easy to love people who love you back. What about the people placed in your life who are hard to love? I know that we all can relate to this. It could be that person at your job who seems as if she makes it her daily mission to aggravate you and get you mad. It's like she is purposely trying to push all of your buttons. What about the neighbor who plays loud music at night when you are trying to relax and get some sleep? Or when you are driving to work with your worship music on, and you're singing, giving glory to God, "Hallelujah." Then somebody cuts you off! What is your reaction? I could be singing "Holy, Holy, Holy," and someone may cut me off, and my reaction may not always be good—something like, "Look at this idiot!" I'm getting better now, and instead I try to stay calm and practice patience. Walking in the Spirit does not make for an easy walk, because we are warring against the flesh. It takes making a decision to walk with God and asking Him to help you, willfully taking one step at a time with the Holy Spirit leading the way.

It's only by the grace of God that we are able to live lives full of the power of Christ. In your flesh you may want to get back at the coworker who is making your day almost intolerable. In your flesh you may want to say a few choice words to her, but the Spirit will prompt you not to. I was in my flesh when I got angry at the reckless driver and called him a name under my breath, with a quick "Lord, please forgive me" at the end. It's all about choices. We have a choice to walk in the Spirit or fulfill the lust of the flesh (Gal. 5:16). There is a kind of tug-of-war going on: the Spirit against the flesh, and we have to choose which side we are on. On one side you have the flesh, and heading up that team is Satan and sometimes us. Sometimes we just want to do what we want to do. We are enticed by our desires (James 1:14). Now the works of the flesh are evident, which are: "adultery, fornication, uncleanness, lewdness, idolatry, sorcery, hatred, contentions, jealousies, outbursts of wrath, selfish ambitions, dissensions, heresies, envy, murders, drunkenness, revelries, and the like" (Gal. 5:19). On the other side, you have the fruit of the Spirit, being led by Christ:

"love, joy, peace, longsuffering, kindness, goodness, faithfulness, gentleness, and self-control" (Gal. 5:22–23). These two sides are warring against each other. It's your choice to pick a side. If you stay in the middle, you still lose. Each decision is pulling you closer to one of the sides. Your life and eternal destination depends on what side you choose. Choosing God's side enables you to win in life now and ensures your life with God eternally.

In a game of tug-of-war, you fall sometimes, and such is life. We fall, God picks us back up, and we try again. In this tug-of-war, Christ is before you, pulling for you, and also in the back pulling for you; He is your rear guard (Isa. 52:12). With Christ you cannot lose. He upholds your steps so that you won't slip. (Psalm 17:5) Endeavor to always set Him before you and you will not be moved. (Psalm 16:8) It is He that arms you with strength, and makes your way perfect. (Psalm 18:32) The word of the Lord is proven; and He is a shield to all who trust Him. (Psalm 18:30)

I encourage you to trust Him with all of your heart. No matter how dim your life may seem to get His light is able to penetrate and make a way. God takes care of His children and He is always with you. He's always with you so be sure you spend time with Him. Linger long in His glorious presence and allow Him to saturate you with His love, joy, peace and power. Your faith will grow, your relationship with God will deepen, and your life will be transformed by His glory, for His glory.

Encourage yourself in His word. Pray always. Open up your heart to Him and be honest before Him in humility. Surrendering your will for His will. Go forward in the strength of the Lord. I pray that God will send His word to your every area of need. Every promise of God is His will. When we pray according to His will, and live according to His will, we can be effective in our prayers and we will experience His promises manifested in our lives for His glory. A life hidden in Him is a life that will have prevailing prayers. To God be the glory.

"If you abide in Me, and My words abide in you, you will ask what you desire, and it shall be done for you. By this My Father is glorified" (John:15:7-8a)

Prayer Matter

Father, in the name of Jesus, I thank You for my life. I thank You for always leading me to triumph in Christ (2 Cor. 2:14[a]). I thank You for being my High Priest and My Hiding Place. I thank You for the awesome privilege for my life to be hidden with Christ in You. In You is where I long to be. In You is peace, tranquility, and an ever-flowing, abundant stream of Your Precious Love. You are my life. I pray that every fragment of my life be hidden in You. If there are any areas that are exposed, reveal them to me, and give me strength by Your Spirit to do the things that I need to do to be completely in Your will.

Father, may Your love flow through me to others. I know a life genuinely hidden in You will show love and concern for other people. Just as you lived a self-sacrificial life, grow me to get beyond myself and to seek opportunities to be a blessing to someone. Give me a genuine love for people. Where I want to stay to myself or be antisocial, free me to be more outgoing and have sincere concern for others. Help me to be more proactive in being a servant. Strengthen me to always respond to others in a way that brings You glory. Loving and serving Your people is an honor and I want my heart and spirit to be in perfect unity with Yours so that Your love can be shown through me in a way that they know that it's love from above.

Where I have been disobedient, I ask for Your forgiveness. Help me to live a life in obedience to You. I thank You for Your conviction and I pray that I will always respond quickly with a repentant heart. Help me not to yield to the power of my flesh. I pray that my love for You will be so strong that I will never want to grieve You. Help me to grow in Your sufficient grace. I thank You that Your strength is made perfect in my weakness (2 Cor. 12:9). I give You glory Lord, for in You have I found deliverance. I thank You that the yoke of bondage is destroyed because of the anointing. (Isa. 10:27b)

I thank You for the opportunity to have a new life and union with You. I seek You with all my heart, all of my mind, and all of my soul. Lord, I ask that You would strengthen me and give me endurance to run the race that you have set before me. I ask for a mighty outpouring of Your Spirit upon me. May the fullness of Your Holy Spirit released enable me to live a powerful life for Your glory. May I rejoice to the extent that I partake in Your sufferings, that when Your glory is revealed, I may also be glad with exceeding joy (1 Pet. 4:13).

May my heart be set on things above and not on things on this earth. Teach me to walk more in the Spirit, to walk more in Your ways. Free me from any spirit of rebellion that wants to do my own thing or go my own way.

Lord, I yield all that I am to You in complete abandonment to my will. I pray that Your will be done in my life on earth as it is in heaven. I give You my heart, my life, my everything. From now on, I will run to You with everything that is within me. I refuse to give up. I'm determined to allow You to have Your way with me. I can do nothing without You, but with You, all things are possible (Phil. 4:13)! You have shown Yourself so strong and so mighty in my life. There are no words to describe how I feel in my heart and how my spirit overflows with thanks and gratitude to You. I thank You for touching my life in such a special way, and as I continue to allow You to perfect me, I ask that You be glorified in me. I surrender myself to be used to touch the hearts of others for You. My Everlasting Father, I love You. I ask You to continue to teach me how to serve You, teach me how to pray. In Jesus's name I pray, amen.

Prayer Matters

Made in the USA
Monee, IL
04 February 2023